GOD IN SEARCH OF MAN

GOD IN SEARCH OF MAN

by

Marie-Abdon Santaner, O.F.M.Cap.

Translated by

Ruth C. Douglas

NEWMAN PRESS

Westminster, Md.   New York, N. Y.   Glen Rock, N. J.

Amsterdam   Toronto   Montreal

A Newman Press edition, originally published under the title *Dieu cherche l'homme,* © Editions Ouvrieres, 1966, Paris, France.

NIHIL OBSTAT:
Robert E. Hunt, S.T.D.
Censor Librorum

IMPRIMATUR:
✠ Thomas A. Boland, S.T.D.
Archbishop of Newark

February 6, 1968

Library of Congress
Catalog Card Number: 68-21458

Published by Newman Press
Editorial Office: 304 W. 58th St., N.Y., N.Y. 10019
Business Office: Westminster, Maryland 21157

Printed and bound in the
United States of America

Contents

Introduction

"At the beginning of his conversion Francis wanted to stand naked before the Bishop. . . ."

Saint Bonaventure

In Scripture the experience lived on earth by every man commences with the story of original sin. This tale is particularly suggestive in its details of the events that followed the fault (cf. Gen. 3, 7-10).

"Then the eyes of both were opened, and they knew that they were naked; and they sewed fig leaves together and made themselves aprons.

"And they heard the sound of the Lord God walking in the garden in the cool of the day, and the man and his wife hid themselves from the presence of the Lord God among the trees of the garden."

A. Every man as Adam hides himself and of every man, as of Adam, God asks, "Where are you?"
"And the man and his wife hid themselves. . . ." All men since Adam have known, know, and will know this instinctive need to hide themselves.

As soon as the years of childhood have passed away, man surprises himself one day in the act of hiding. This is the day when his eyes are opened on himself. And after the first little lie has been uttered by his childish lips, a series of contrivances is developed, each one more cunning than the other. He finds he is capable of using them to hide himself as he advances into life.

There are of course, the real lies, in word and in deed; these we avoid as much as possible. But there are also the lies that are not recognized as such—the "strategic" evasions of the strong and the wily, the manifestations of aggressivity of the weak and the stupid. There are calculated diversions and unconscious compensations. The

1

technique employed is of no importance; the essential is to hide oneself.

"Adam and his wife hid themselves . . ."

Now while we are hidden, each one of us preoccupied only with avoiding the unpleasantness of being discovered "naked," the Lord God, without noise or fanfare, causes his footfalls to be heard. In the garden, that is our human existence, God walks "in the cool of the day."

As soon as peaceful calm, represented here by the "cool of the day," is reestablished in a man, that is, when the ascendancy of his surroundings or of his prejudices, the fascination of his ideas or of his dreams, the giddiness produced by his activities and above all by his successes, have all relaxed their hold on him, then at the very heart of his life, he hears the sound of the Lord walking and calling him: "The Lord God called to Adam: 'Where are you?' "

When in sacred scripture the Lord God asks Adam this question, it is not that he ignores or pretends to ignore in which corner of the garden or behind what bushes Adam and his wife had hidden themselves. The question is a call for renewal of that dialogue which God, before sin, had held familiarly with man.

The first man thinks that this dialogue is broken. Surprised by the discovery of his nudity, his only thought is to hide. God, however, wishes to resume and carry on this dialogue.

The words, "Where are you?" are the first words God addresses to man after sin. These words open the history of the relationship between God and man, the sinner. They are also its summation. The relationship between God and man, whether on the level of the collective life of humanity or on the level of the personal existence of each individual, is, as far as God is concerned, a constant solicitation for the renewal of a dialogue. "The Lord called to Adam: 'Where are you?' "

B. As Adam, we can reply to the question only by admitting our nakedness and fear.

"I heard the sound of thee in the garden, and I was afraid, because I was naked and I hid myself."

These are the first words that scripture places on the lips of the first man after the first fall. Placing these words of Adam on our own lips can allow us to understand their mysterious significance. As Adam and Eve, men hide themselves *because they are afraid.*

All men seek to overcome the instinctive reaction of fear aroused in the depths of their being by each new ray of light projected on it by the trials of existence; all try to find the security of some "hiding place," a protective coloration.

This coloration, whose only function is to anesthetize us against fear, is complex and diverse.

The esteem, the approval, the connivence, and, if need be, the complicity of others . . . the ideas we nurture and cherish about ourselves and that we will defend even by falling ill if necessary . . . the evasions and distractions, and the occupations and preoccupations with which we pretend to be overwhelmed."

The question, "Where are you?" endangers all these securities where we make "hiding places." Above all, it threatens those securities we like to characterize as religious or supernatural to delude ourselves the better on their real value.

The man who wants to answer the question, "Where are you?" can only do so truthfully if he consents to make his own the confession of Adam: "I have hidden myself." He must, even if he is not conscious of it, admit in advance and identify the existence all around him of a whole bundle of illusions, perhaps of lies, a whole surrounding of trees and bushes that form a reassuring screen for his fear-haunted being.

Without this confession, man, collectively as well as individually, cannot renew an authentic dialogue with God.

C. To every man as to Adam God gives the true answer: "You have eaten."

"God said: 'Who told you that you were naked? Have you eaten of the tree of which I commanded you not to eat?' The man said: 'The woman whom thou gavest to be with me, she gave me the fruit of the tree and I ate . . .' The woman said, 'The serpent beguiled me . . .' "

In this scene Adam and Eve have only one thing on their minds— the assessment of responsibilities. The Lord God is far above the thought of responsibilities to be divided and judgments to be uttered. He observes "Have you not eaten?" Man has eaten; that is, something has entered into him and now forms one body with him. This "something," man carries *in his blood* from now on.

Collectively and individually, man would be only too prone like Adam and Eve to reserve for himself as a last resort the paltry security of a finger pointed at someone more guilty than himself. "It is the woman . . ." "It is the snake . . ."

But to enter into dialogue with God is not to bring him additional information for the completion of a just sentence. Even less is it to undertake personally the trial of someone else, be it spouse or companion (it is the woman). Nor can this dialogue be joined in the indictment of some obscure influence, evil in general or the devil, who is sometimes most convenient (it is the snake).

To enter into dialogue with God is to welcome the truth. The biblical text in which the stages of this entry into dialogue are noted gives us its conditions. We must admit the existence of fear at the vital center of our being. We must stop anesthetizing ourselves against this fear and consent to experience it. We must draw a lesson from this fear and to do this, we must welcome God's words. Between God and ourselves a dialogue will be established if we accept the truth.

Conclusions: To be clothed by God in Jesus Christ we must give ourselves to the Word of God that lays us bare.

"At the beginning of his conversion Francis of Assisi wished to stand naked before the Bishop . . ."

By this gesture inspired in him by God, the Poverello not only expressed the will to detach himself from all earthly goods he also affirmed his resolution to expect henceforth his security from God alone as from a Father. Indeed, God alone can *clothe* man.

The story of the first fault tells us this in its own way. "The Lord God made for Adam and for his wife garments of skins and he clothed them." To those who admit their fears and consent to recognize their inner nakedness God gives tunics of skins. It is for them that the fleece of the lamb has been woven. Hanging naked on the tree of the cross, the lamb of God has made of his own blood the one and only garment that can deliver man from his state of nudity. Henceforth, to gain acceptance from God, man needs nothing other than the love with which God has loved him in his Son, Christ Jesus. He who avails himself of this love shall no longer fear (cf. 1 Jn. 17, 18); he knows himself to be clothed by God in the garment that restores him to his original right: Jesus Christ (cf. Eph. 4, 24; Col. 3, 10, 1 Cor. 4, 10—5, 5).

It is worth ridding ourselves of all our illusions to obtain such a blessing. Illusions may reassure us about ourselves, but they leave us in our nakedness. To put on Jesus Christ, we must give ourselves without reservation to the Word that lays us bare.

"For the word of God is living and active, sharper than any two edged sword." Today we would say that it is more incisive than a scalpel.

"Piercing to the division of soul and spirit, of joints and marrow." It separates pitilessly in us the conscious from the unconscious, the motives and the motivations, that which is free from that which is enslaved; it screens our attitudes and our patterns of behavior, "discerning the thoughts and intentions of the heart," knowing how to distinguish between the role we are playing and the persons we really are.

"And before him no creature is hidden, but all are open and laid bare to the eyes of him with whom we have to do" (Heb. 12, 13).

So that the dialogue that can deliver us may be established between God and ourselves, let us lend him our ears and listen to his voice. "The Lord God called man: 'Where are you?' "

REFLECTIONS ON THE INTRODUCTORY THEME

A. POINTS FOR MEDITATION

1. I must answer the Lord's query: "Where are you?" No one can be sure that his reply is objective and that it proceeds from an exact awareness of self. Each one of us fluctuates between excessive

hatred and excessive love of self. A right conscience has nothing to do with all that.

2. I have a certain intuition of the fear that is working within me but nothing more. This intuition is expressed through attitudes and especially through the reflex of self-justification. Examples of self-justification at the time of beginning a retreat: "A retreat? What's the use? I know myself well enough. As for changing myself . . . I already know what I have to do."

3. These reflexes of self-justification are the signs of my fear. Fear of what? This is what has to be made clear. It is not in the midst of noise and agitation that clarity can be made. Noise and agitation are the equivalents of flight.

B. Texts for Reading and Prayer

a. Biblical Texts

Is. 5, 16-25. Return to the truth.
Ezek. 16. The entire chapter. All being and all possessions are gifts received from God.
Job 4, 13-20. The human heart stripped bare.
2 Cor. 5, 1-12. The only vestment desirable for man.
Lk. 15, 18-19. The prodigal son wants to justify himself. He does not yet "know" his Father (v. 22).

b. Books

Thomas of Celano, *Vita Prima,* Part I, chaps. 1-6.
St. Francis, *First Letter.*

c. Prayers

Ps. 32. Only a humble confession frees us.
Ps. 42, 43. Desire and fear of God, then act of hope.
Ps. 139. Homage to God who explores the depths of man's heart.
Ps. 130. Confidence in the Lord who does not judge, but forgives.
Ps. 62. God, the only help on which man can always rely.

Final Theme

Eph. 3, 12.

PART ONE
Our Personal Nature

I

To Allow Oneself To Be Overcome

> "The sight of the lepers was too bitter for me to behold."
>
> St. Francis of Assisi. *Testament*

"YOU HAVE STRIVEN WITH GOD."

A. Human destiny, individual and collective, foreshadowed in Jacob's combat. One of the most mysterious passages in scripture is the one that tells us the story of Jacob's struggle with God (cf. Gen. 32).

"The same night he arose and took his two wives, his two maids, and his eleven children, and crossed the ford of Jabbok. He took them and sent them across the stream, and likewise everything that he had.

"And Jacob was left alone; and a man wrestled with him until the breaking of the day. When the man saw that he did not prevail against Jacob, he touched the hollow of his thigh; and Jacob's thigh was put out of joint as he wrestled with him. Then he said, 'Let me go, for the day is breaking.' But Jacob said, 'I will not let you go, unless you bless me.' And he said to him, 'What is your name?' And he said, 'Jacob.' Then he said, 'Your name shall no more be called Jacob, but Israel, for you have striven with God and with men, and have prevailed.' Then Jacob asked him, 'Tell me, I pray, your name.' But he said, 'Why is it that you ask my name?' And there he blessed him. So Jacob called the name of the place Penuel, saying, 'For I have seen God face to face, and yet my life is preserved.'

"The sun rose upon him as he passed Penuel, limping because of his thigh."

One brief detail alone in the above text should suffice to convince us that it deserves our closest scrutiny. Jacob receives a new name,

9

the name under which all those called by God to be his people will group themselves—Israel. When God, in scripture, gives a name, it foreshadows an entire destiny.

Thus, in Cephas (stone, rock), the name given by Christ to Simon, son of Jonas, is a prefiguration of the destiny of the immovable rock upon which the Church of Christ has its foundation.

The name, Israel, also foreshadows an entire destiny: the fate of a people against whom the Almighty has struggled for almost four thousand years. And truly is this people named Israel (striven with God) because after centuries of battle, the Almighty has not yet emerged victorious.

But from this combat, Israel has come forth crippled, limping from a wounded thigh. All through history and down into our own times, we can follow step by step, through persecutions, deportations, concentration camps, pogroms, and gas ovens, the road along which the nation once born of Jacob hobbles.

Now whatever is written of Israel, whatever befalls Israel is figurative (cf. 1 Cor. 10, 6. 11). We ourselves live the reality.

The mysterious struggle from which Jacob, the first Israel, emerges wounded foreshadows our own destiny, individually as well as collectively. We strive against God, we, too, resist him all our lives, but just as Jacob was bruised during his struggle, so we, too, are hurt each time we resist; we, too, are wounded in that mysterious part of our being where our conduct, attitudes, behavior, and actions themselves are rooted and articulated.

B. Our will to independence is   ". . . a man wrestled with him
   directed against God himself.   until the breaking of the day,"
                                        says the text.

As man enters conscious life, the darkness of existence here on earth thickens around him.

Here ends the transparency of all things that were the joy of childhood. Now everything becomes a problem. Essentially, the teenager is being disturbed by this progressive darkening. From now on, he must advance in the dark (cf. Rom. 13, 12), and the darkness will persist until the light of eternity finally shines upon him.

But in this darkness that has made his world opaque man perceives a presence. Someone is there. And this presence cannot be evaded. To be a man is to become aware of this face to face confrontation. To the same degree that man is truly conscious of his own existence, he is mindful of the mysterious presence of this "someone." But for this to occur, he must first of all accept to be himself. Like Jacob at the ford of Jabbok, he must be alone. The unknown will only manifest himself to man when he *is without any other support but that of the reality of his own human condition.*

The unknown, our text tells us, is the true, living God who created man. This living God not only lives but is possessed by the desire to communicate his life. This living God created man so that he could be enabled to live the divine life. And this living God is actively seeking him. For in man, drawn out of dust by his living Word, the living God seeks a place in which to sow the seed of divine life, which is spirit (cf. 1 Pet. 1, 23).

An encounter between man born of earth, and God who is inaccessible light, could only be a face to face confrontation which would plunge man into darkness. But in the midst of this obscurity man struggled; Adam's refusal of grace turned the encounter into a combat, and ever since then in this age old struggle, each man has been an Israel; he has striven with God.

We strive with God with all the fragility of a freedom that is in its formative stage only, a freedom that seeks much more than it possesses itself.

We strive with God with resistances of all kinds rising up within us and blocking the way to aspirations in which the best part of our being would like to express itself.

We especially strive with God with the strength of the servitude of sin and all its consequences weighing heavily upon us and handicapping us—inherited tendencies, atavistic leanings toward evil, ingrown habits. All these are just so many points of resistance which allow us to remain distant from God during the struggle he wages unceasingly against us.

God freely offers to communicate his life and thus equality with himself to each one of us. Yet the sinner in us opposes it. We feel ourselves made for this equality, but we want to owe it to ourselves alone. God's loving approach is regarded as a violation of our right to choose our own destinies. "Father, give me the share of property that falls to me," is the request of the prodigal son to his father (Lk. 15, 12).

From such a dark web of circumstances, we spontaneously adopt a defensive attitude toward God as if he were an aggressor. Thus, almost any event in our lives can become for us an angel of the Lord whom we resist; we oppose God. But we emerge wounded from each conflict and the more we remove ourselves from the promptings of grace, the deeper our wounds. Man thinks he is safeguarding his own nature, his very being, but in reality, he keeps diminishing that which most truly leads him to be himself—his own free will. "When the man saw that he did not prevail against Jacob, he touched the hollow of his thigh; and Jacob's thigh was put out of joint as he wrestled with him."

C. Every resistance to the Lord brings about in ourselves the degradation of that which truly makes us human. The degradation of our being, wounded in its innermost depths, is attributed to the Lord: "He touched the hollow of his thigh."

There are numerous setbacks and trials in the history of Israel and they are invariably presented to us as chastisements visited upon Israel by the Lord. "You have rejected me, says the Lord, you keep going backward; so I have stretched out my hand against you and destroyed you; I am weary of relenting" (Jer. 15, 6; cf. also vv. 13, 20, 27). These passages, as a hundred others, attribute sentiments of human vengeance to God. We must try to understand their real meaning.

It is clear that we cannot attribute directly to God, the ruination that fell upon Israel as a series of punishments. Theologically speaking, it would simply be inadmissible. But scripture, in attributing Israel's ruination to God, is expressing in halting, primitive terms a profound theological truth. It tells us that to try to escape God is necessarily fatal to Israel, just as much as if the God of vengeance himself demanded an accounting from his People.

Now Israel is the figure of our human condition, individually and collectively.

This is the true meaning of the indignities and trials which may have pressed heavily upon us: They are not direct punishments from God. When man withdraws from God, there is no need for God to intervene directly. The very fact that he has violated the natural order established by God is sufficient to bring upon him situations fraught with suffering that he will have to bear. Man's very nature is, so to speak, delivered unto the forces of disintegration that he unleashes each time he refuses to obey his own inner law. "Your wickedness will chasten you and your apostasy will reprove you. Know and see that it is evil and bitter for you to forsake the Lord your God . . . Yet I planted you a choice vine . . . How then have you turned degenerate and become a wild vine?" (Jer. 2, 17. 19.)

Individually or collectively, when man refuses to recognize his dependence on God, he degrades himself. And what is usually called "punishment" is simply the outcome of his refusal to be dependent on God. He has, in fact, dedicated himself to his own degradation.

At times and in certain circumstances, to turn away from or refuse God's will seems the way to be wholly oneself. However, if at times we feel satisfaction, even a sort of exaltation in the acts or attitudes by which we express our independence from God's plan, we always find ourselves ultimately hurt, wounded, or diminished in stature, and in proportion to the intensity of our resistance.

How multiple and various are the degradations we inflict upon ourselves. Individually, there are sterile withdrawals into self, vicious personal habits, rancors and misunderstandings and cultivated hostility to others in which we allow ourselves to vegetate. Collectively, there is selfish pleasure-seeking, group egoism, opposition for the pleasure of opposing, the promotion of hate, underlying conflicts, and destructive wars.

All these degradations which the human race, individually and collectively, inflicts upon itself, derive from the one fundamental degradation that makes man into the unwitting slave of an idol—the image he has created of himself. For this arbitrarily directs his energies, and wastes his inner drives by placing them at the service of an illusion. Man then resists God, thinking that he is defending his own person while in reality he is defending an idol, a myth, the image of himself to which in the most secret sanctuary of his being he has erected an altar.

Conclusions: The dangers of worshipping one's own image. Every man is thus led by an image of himself which he constructs from within by his efforts and attitudes while he seeks, at the same time, the respect and approbation of others: "I'm the sort of man who. . . . You can't persuade me to. . . . I'm not one of those who. . . ."

The power of this image arouses and mobilizes in each one of us the most fundamental drives of our being.

However, as long as we are led by an image of ourselves which we have not sufficiently identified to be able to control, submitting ourselves to God is out of the question. The man who lives for his idol simply cannot conform to God's design for him. To the degree that his self-made image differs from his true nature, from his innermost being, this man by the pursuit of such an image is simply degrading himself.

Grace itself, if he prays for it, will not help him in the way in which he thinks it will. It can only act on the reality of being, not on the shadowy insubstantial figment of his imagination and desires whose existence his behavior is forever trying to prove.

Thus, on the dual plane of nature and grace, to cultivate an image of oneself is already a resistance to, and beginning of a struggle, against God.

By what image of myself am I led?

Before his conversion, Francis of Assisi found that "the sight of lepers was too bitter to behold."

Is my true self the leper which I find too bitter to contemplate?

FIRST REFLECTION ON THE THEME
To Allow Oneself to Be Overcome

A. POINTS FOR MEDITATION

1. In whatever pain or anguish we happen to find ourselves, let it be our rule to seek, not its cause, but its meaning.

2. We are quick to find an explanation for our trials and troubles

in the wickedness or thoughtlessness of others. Rarely do we seek the light which they could shed on ourselves.

3. When we are only half given to God, we are in perpetual, inner torment. It seems unwise therefore to give only half to God. It may be that we would be better off giving him nothing at all.

4. To dream of a life where renouncement would be unnecessary is to dream of an unreal world. Even more so, is it unreal to wish to live in God's service without denying ourselves because this refusal arrests the full development of our being which we could otherwise attain.

5. It is said that grace perfects nature. This is true, but the first aim of grace is not to perfect nature but to save it. For nature, in its present condition, is the prisoner of sin.

6. The profession of atheism is possible for anyone simply because every human being, priests and religious included, is capable of refusing to recognize God as his God.

7. The tragedy of humanistic atheism is but the psychological sum of all individual atheisms, of believers as well as of unbelievers.

8. Can I really affirm before God that for me, he is really God?

9. "I will not let you go unless you bless me," said Jacob to the unknown. Thus, humanity in our time of technical advance expresses in its own fashion man's desire for a blessing, that is, a goal for which it feels itself to be made. By the very activities in which men seem to be opposing or refusing God they show to what degree they are passionately, although blindly seeking him.

"THOU SHALT PREVAIL AGAINST MEN. . . ."

A. To allow ourselves to be possessed by God means that first of all we must be able to possess ourselves. ". . . you have striven with God . . ." said the Lord to Jacob at the end of the night's struggle. During our night here below we, too, strive with God: "We are a true Israel, a stiff-necked people" (cf. Deut. 9, 6).

As with Jacob, our resistances cause us to be wounded but nevertheless like Jacob, we say to the unknown, "I will not let you go unless you bless me." Indeed, even in the acts and the behavior by which it seeks to escape God, our humanity reveals itself to be desiring him passionately. In its errors and its sins our being pursues and strives to obtain a blessing, that is, an attainment for which it feels itself to be made.

In this way the story of Jacob's combat brings us a double assurance. First of all, the assurance that even in the midst of our failings we are in quest of the Lord. Second, that for his part, until that hour when the night will end for us, the Lord will not cease his hand to hand combat with our being.

This double assurance is confirmed again by the affirmation that he has prevailed against men. By this promise to Jacob, we as creatures receive from the living God a sort of advance guarantee that the combat waged here below will have a happy ending.

The reflection inspired by this text is of capital importance for it concerns our attitudes toward God.

We have already seen that because of our sinful condition, we feel defensive about God's overtures to us. However we suspect or feel his presence—we may feel it intuitively—we may easily mistake it as aggressive because we are born of Adam. Now we should be in a position to welcome him.

How can we maintain intact in ourselves the willingness to be seized and possessed by God? We can foresee at once the necessity for self-possession and the importance of the disciplinary action of self-acting on self to submit to his action. Through the images of

16

the combat of Jacob we see formulated a dialectic of nature and grace. At the price of self-effort, the life we receive freely from God must be able to act in us (cf. Phil. 2, 12; Mt. 11, 12). St. Paul, the apostle, who gives the most attention to the affirmation of the gratuity of God's gift, is also the apostle who most categorically reminds us of the necessity of efforts on our part.

"Yield yourselves to God as men who have been brought from death to life and your members to God as instruments of righteousness" (Rom. 6, 13).

To the Corinthians, he confides the struggle by which he endeavors to submit his entire being (1 Cor. 9, 24. 27).

An ill-informed confidence in grace sometimes induces the Christian not to be concerned enough with the realities of nature. Now nature is scarred by the burden of sin. It has its own imperatives. To ignore them is no proof of faith but it is to expect of God miracles that he will not accomplish.

It is therefore not enough to proclaim in word and resolution our consent to God's plan for us. We need an entire policy for ourselves in the highest sense of that word, which is to say that we must take hold of the tumultuous beings that we are to submit to God.

To be the master of one's body, senses, and imagination requires a disciplined life. At the minimum it demands the control of sense impressions and of the images which fill our subconscious. It also demands the asceticism of hard work, healthful habits in eating, drinking, sleeping, and the cult of the inner life as well as the calm mastery of the instinct of curiosity.

These are elementary requirements. To claim to be submissive to God without satisfying them is to be either very naive or very proud. The naivete is no less fatal than the pride in many cases.

B. To allow oneself to be overcome requires above all else that we first of all "accept" ourselves.

The reminder of these requirements must not mislead us.

The Christian is not being asked to achieve a sort of record performance in self-mastery.

Now one often gets the impression, especially among religious, that Christians of goodwill exhaust themselves trying to fullfill what they call "perfection." They cripple themselves by trying to overcome their nature instead of allowing themselves to be overcome by the God who, because he has created their nature, knows it perfectly and intends above all else to respect it.

To allow oneself to be overcome by God certainly does not mean to become a sort of superman or hero of will power. It does mean, first of all, to be inclined to accept oneself humbly, to accept being short or tall, weak or strong, well balanced or subject to giddiness, just as the great current flowing from the act of creation has brought us into the world.

It is also to accept oneself as being in a situation of becoming, in a condition of perpetual recommencement. We must therefore will to assume serenely, day after day, the events of life. We must refuse in advance the bitter satisfaction of brooding regrets and deliberately establish in ourselves the intention of integrating the entire past (with ourselves or others) of which we are in some way the fruit or result.

To allow oneself to be overcome by God is to condescend to the necessities burdening our human nature that emerged from the earth, and not to aspire to the life of pure spirit when our body and our sensitivity demand their legitimate and indispensable nourishment.

"To allow oneself to be overcome by *God*" is finally *to be human,* to be *oneself.*

In the struggle in which God hems us in on all sides and which he wages unceasingly against us in this world, to be overcome is to renounce cherishing any image of ourselves that we have fabricated.

We must accept ourselves as we are and not play the role of the rich man or the poor man, the intellectual or the ignorant one, the saint or the devil, the ascetic or the man of the world. And we should not try to be proud or humble, but know how to laugh and how to cry.

We must will to be ourselves, not only because we are the final result of millions of years of human development, but also because we are the results of the consequences of our own acts in our past lives.

And we must know how to love ourselves, above all, in moments of awkwardness without ever despising or cursing some personal idiosyncracy, but welcoming ourselves as we would welcome the most pitiful of our brothers.

To allow oneself to be overcome by God is, then, to adopt toward oneself the attitude of God who is overflowing with love for his handiwork.

"But thou art merciful to all, for thou canst do all things . . . For thou lovest all things that exist, and hast loathing for none of the things that thou hast made . . ." (Wis. 11, 23-24. Cf. also Wis. 11, 25—12, 2).

C. The ideal achievement: Mary gives us its perfect example in her fiat. It is only in the measure that man espouses the movement of God toward his creature that he can face the truth about himself and hope not to "have striven with God."

We must renounce strength. We must renounce it individually and collectively. And let us not dwell too much on so-called modern man and his Promethean pretensions. Let us rather think of the quest for influence and of the rivalry between religious orders and communities, of the mirages of success or of self-perfection so readily ennobled by those who pursue them in the name of contemplation or the apostolate.

Now the Lord asks us, collectively and individually, to consent to the truth about our being, "weak" in its origins and weakened still further by the ferment of corruption which we have "eaten" in Adam. "You have striven with . . . men, and have prevailed," said the Lord to Jacob after having given him the name of Israel. To prevail against men is to tear oneself away from the exaggeration which has blinded man and prevented him from being truly himself. It has falsified the normal chain of relationships between God and himself and has transformed into a combat what was to have been an alliance.

There was a single moment in the history of the universe when a human being achieved the balance of sanity, an instant when all creation attained in a young girl of fifteen an ultimate degree of self expression. Creation said, "Yes" in this child by giving itself in her to the personal outpouring of the Word. All the exaggerated dreams, the products of human imagination expressed in myth and legend, found at this hour an accomplishment that surpassed them as much as the heavens surpass the earth (cf. Is. 55). It was the entire human race throbbing with unrequited desires that expressed itself in the silent consent that Mary gave to *God's* plan for her. In this fragment of living dust that was the virgin, the Word of God was able to become dust without troubling or altering anything in Mary, so perfect was the consent that this daughter of men gave to the plans of *God,* so complete was the harmony between the aspirations that she nourished in her heart and the outpouring in her of the Word of *God.* In Mary, unison existed between the effusion of divine tenderness on its created work and the response given by the creature to the will of God on her. That which was rejected by the first Adam as an intrusion into the domain of his freedom, the mother of the new Adam wished to accept wholeheartedly. In advance, she wants to be entirely that which the gift that is given her is to make of her." How can this be since I have no husband?" She is not asking for explanations. She only wishes to know what is expected of her. She does not argue. She is only too sure that her fidelity to God will fulfill her deepest expectations far more abundantly than anything that she could conceive or imagine herself (cf. Eph. 3, 20).

The primitive Church made no mistakes about this. By saluting spontaneously in her who had thus given herself up to God whose creation she was the privilege of a virginity matching the self-transcendence, that is, the bringing into the world of a new being, the Church pays homage to the perfect availability that the will of God found in Mary and to the perfect harmony between the wishes of God and the deep expectations of the Virgin.

Conclusions: The price of a true knowledge of self, the fruit of silence kept in the face of self. It is because he does not know well enough the true expectations of his human nature that man is the victim of the disproportion of his dreams, and is condemned to show himself to strive with God, strong with a strength that is, in fact, only the difficulty he has in keeping himself lovingly available to the initiatives of the living God.

By making us alive with his own life, this living God would have us become wholly ourselves. He would deliver us without altering us; he would make us fruitful without deteriorating us; he would recreate us in his own supernature without ceasing to create us according to the law of our own nature.

We are able to understand here how only total availability to God can allow man to avoid being obliged to leave the theater of his successive combats "wounded until dawn," that is, until the end of his night here below. But this total availability can only proceed from a deep self-knowledge which is not abstract, nor a result of learning. It cannot even come of psychological learning. It requires us to learn to keep ourselves attentive to the Word of God that is our own personal nature, the Word by which God is continually creating us.

The benefits, for which this attitude is the condition, are tremendous. On the collective as on the individual level, in the assumption of universal responsibilities as well as in the conduct of the most strictly personal aspects of life it is the only way to save the whole man. It is therefore worth man's effort to oblige himself resolutely to be attentive to this Word of God that is his own nature. But every man must be determined in advance to hear this Word formulate itself not as he would wish it but as it really does pronounce itself in the truth of his being.

Such is the basic disposition from which man can hope to prevail against men. "The Lord led me amongst lepers," writes Francis of Assisi in his *Testament*. Let us allow ourselves to be led by the Lord among those "traits" of our being that we have systematically refused to recognize up until now. Beyond these traits and to the truest and deepest part of ourselves the Lord wishes to lead us.

SECOND REFLECTION ON THE THEME
To Allow Oneself To Be Overcome

A. POINTS FOR MEDITATION

1. Every man is led by an image of himself which he constructs by his own efforts. As long as this image leads him without being identified and controlled by him, he will be a slave of his own dream, and will simply not be able to discern God's inspirations nor conform himself to them.

2. A man can spend his life fleeing from himself, or rather fleeing from the reality of himself which he cannot resign himself to recognize. This is the case of whoever labors under a false image of his self which he wants to prove to himself or to others.

3. If the image I have of myself does not correspond to my true nature, to my innermost being, when I pursue the fulfillment of this image I subvert my nature. I am really fighting against God, from whom my nature comes.

4. The man who will not accept himself in the reality of his created being cannot enter into a dialogue with God the Creator. He must accept the real conditions of his life and his existence in this world as the only basis from which we can progress toward the full growth of divine life in himself and in others.

5. The reactions of others echo back to me the impressions I unconsciously form of myself. These reactions, even when they are unjust, can enlighten me. My family, my professional surroundings, my social environment, the places where I live or re-create, are all messengers of God for me.

B. PARTICULAR THEMES

Priests. A priest forms an image of his ministry, his function, and his person. What is this image? At what time did it take shape? Does it correspond to the real world?

Religious. Is there not a saint somewhere whose traits we are trying to reproduce? At what period did this saint live? What was his or her temperament, his activities, or social environment? We must not "mimic" the saints but inspire ourselves with their examples.

Parents. What image do we have of the relationship we should have with our children? Where did we find the components of this image?

C. TEXTS FOR READING AND PRAYER

a. Biblical Texts

Gen. 1—2, 4. God is filled with wonderment. "Everything in his work is very good."
Wis. 11, 22—12, 3. Solicitude of God for his work.

Ecclus. 1-7 and passim. Wisdom is in a healthy equilibrium.

2 Cor. 4; 5; 6. Combats carried on by Paul in the truth. See also I Thess. 2; 2 Tim. 2, 1-24.

Lk. 15, 13. The son could not go into a more faraway country than that state in which he had ceased to be himself, the son of his father.

b. Books

Thomas of Celano, *Vita Prima*. Part I, chaps. 15 and 19.
St. Francis. *Admonitions*.

c. Prayers

Ps. 12. May God deliver us from lies.

Ps. 80. The variations of Israel—images and foreshadows of our resistances to the truth. For the same see Ps. 106.

Ps. 7. Words one ought to be able to say.

Ps. 101. The loyalty that God loves. See also Pss. 4; 6; 9; 10.

Final Theme

Rom. 12, 1.

II

Into the Wilderness

"Francis, learn to despise thyself if thou wilt know
me. When thou hast made this change in thyself,
thou wilt taste in full the meaning of my words."
Words of Christ to Francis of Assisi
Celano, *Life*

"I WILL BRING HER INTO THE WILDERNESS. . . ."

A. As he did with Israel, God leads every man into the wilderness. These words of the Lord from the second chapter of Hosea (verse 14) are often quoted at the beginning of a retreat. "I will bring her into the wilderness."

Preachers and spiritual writers speculate on these words as they underline the necessity for silence and solitude in the steps that take man to his encounter with God.

Indeed, when God wanted to take Israel away from the servitude of Egypt and into the freedom of the promised land, "he led his people through the wilderness." (Ps. 136, 16)

Now the things that happened to the Israelites "happened to them as a warning but they were written down for our instruction" (1 Cor. 10, 11). What we read about them in scripture is reproduced with far greater reality in the sacred history of the life of every human being.

In other words, just as they were obliged to march forty years in the wilderness before they reached the repose of the promised land, so must each man, a true Israel, accept himself during his entire adult life span as being in a state of journeying through a wilderness. What, therefore, is this wilderness?

24

Perhaps in reaction to the bustle, the noise, and the stifling atmosphere of the cities, we have a tendency to identify the wilderness with some oasis of silence, peace, greenness, and freshness. A "nice quiet corner" sheltered from troublesome intruders.

Let us admit that in the scriptures there are many passages to corroborate this tendency.

In keeping the remembrance of the passage through the wilderness, Israel did not neglect to embellish and idealize this episode, just as the adult whose difficult younger years seem more appealing as he grows further away from them. Six hundred years after the events, Deuteronomy recalls the wilderness days as days of ease, happiness, and glory. "You shall remember . . . the signs, the wonders, the mighty hand and the outstretched arm, by which the Lord your God brought you out" (Deut. 7, 19). "Where there was no water (your God) brought you water out of the flinty rock, who fed you in the wilderness with manna which your fathers did not know" (Deut. 8, 15.16).

The author of the Book of Wisdom, writing from a perspective of almost eleven centuries later, gives an impression of redoubled enthusiasm (cf. Wis. 11, 2. 4). The 114th and 115th Psalms ("In exitu") are a wonderful illustration of the glamor with which this journey was invested in the memory of Israel. "The mountains skip like rams, the hills like lambs."

But in reading the Book of Exodus, whose composition was much closer to the events, we see that the entry into the wilderness was far from accompanied by enthusiasm. Chapters 14, 15, and 16 give us, almost in continuity, some characteristic echoes from the mind of Israel as it entered into the wilderness.

". . . they said to Moses, 'is it because there are no graves in Egypt that you have taken us away to die in the wilderness?' " (Exod. 14, 11). "The people murmured against Moses, saying, 'What shall we drink?' " (Exod. 15, 24). "The people of Israel . . . said . . . 'Would that we had died by the hand of the Lord in the land of Egypt, when we sat by the fleshpots and ate bread to the full' " (Exod. 16, 3).

These are the true facts! The wilderness frightened the Hebrews. As they were about to enter it, they sensed its insecurity, the lack of water, the lack of food. They went on only because the sea, closing in behind them, did not allow them to turn back. They went on because the miracles—the bread from heaven, the water, the column of fire during the night and the cloud that covered them by day—made their march possible. It is therefore normal that the wilderness toward which God leads us should cause us apprehension rather than attract and charm us. Ordinarily, it should be painful for us to enter it.

B. The true wilderness toward Here we must be guided by the
which God leads man is the general context of the scripture.
truth about himself. In the scriptures the wilderness
is not a place of quiet satisfaction and of comfort, not even of spiritual comfort. The wilderness is, above all, the wages of sin.

"Cursed is the ground because of you," said the Lord God to Adam who had just disobeyed him (Gen. 3, 17).

It is evident that the malediction does not fall upon the earth that can't help what happened. This malediction expresses one fact. By withdrawing himself from God, man has become a wilderness. And all through his life he must recognize and accept this fact and the truth about himself.

Israel, loath to enter the land of insecurity, the land of hunger and thirst, now appears as the image and prefiguration of ourselves (individual or group). Instinctively, we all back away when we feel a situation developing that would lead us to see more of the truth about ourselves.

The truth about ourselves! There you have it! This is the true wilderness, of which the Lord speaks when he says, "I will lead her into the wilderness." We are far from the mawkish sentimentality which would see in the divine initiative only the invitation to surround oneself with an empty solitude.

The entire second chapter of Hosea should be read and meditated in this perspective. One will then understand the initiative of God which it expresses without falling into a misconception of the text. "I . . . (will) make her like a wilderness, and set her like a parched land, and slay her with thirst . . . Even clearer and more significant is the image expressed in all its crudity and violence by verse 3: "I (will) strip her naked and make her as the day she was born." "I will hedge her way with thorns; and I will build a wall against her so that she cannot find her paths . . . And I will lay waste her vines and her fig trees" (Hos. 2, 3. 6. 12).

This is the "wilderness" where God leads the man he wishes to conduct into life.

Now just as the wilderness of Sinai frightened the people of Israel so are we, the true Israel, frightened by the wilderness of ourselves (the real wilderness).

Spontaneously, man rediscovers Adam's reflex of covering himself with leaves and hiding among the trees of the earthly paradise. He no more wishes to recognize himself as wilderness than Adam would accept to be naked. Whoever we may be, all of us flee from the wilderness of ourselves.

The rather frequent practice of limiting the exercises of a retreat to the revision of our personal relations with God can thus become the quest for a false wilderness, and the step that leads us into solitude can become the means to flee more surely from the wilderness of self.

C. Condition for entry into the true wilderness: the risk of compensation.

Our concern must therefore be directed to letting the truth possess us and to allowing ourselves to be reduced to complete capitulation, unconditional surrender.

Now truth can only possess us and submit us to itself by starting its work from our own thoughts, that is, from our own lives and the situations they hold in store for us.

" 'The commandment which I command you this day is not too hard for you,' said the Lord to Israel, 'neither is it far off. It is not in heaven, that you should say, "Who will go up for us to heaven, and bring it to us that we may hear it and do it." But the Word is very near you; it is in your mouth and in your heart, so that you can do it' " (Deut. 30, 11. 14).

In this text God tells us how to discover the truth. We are not to suppress the problems of everyday life for a few hours or a few days in the hope of finding him in the heavens or beyond the seas. What we must do is find out in what respect our everyday life is only emptiness, or at the least how it remains empty of God.

This presupposes that we have the will to enter the wilderness, the one that is real, without falsification or sham.

Now every man lies to himself (cf. Rom. 3, 4.) This is not a pessimistic remark but the humble observation that no one can guarantee to himself that he is sure of his own honesty towards himself in the examination he undertakes by himself of his own life. By wishing to be alone, man is much less certain of being truthful in his interpretation of the events of his existence. And in this solitude, he is more apt to mistake his flight from the truth for attachment to it. This is normal.

It is frequently encountered in religious, in whom it is the most frequent form of what the psychologists call compensation.

Compensation can be reduced to a very simple psychological mechanism. Someone has a vague notion of the emptiness or falsity of some of his own attitudes, choices, activities, and ideas. Although it remains on the level of the unconscious this vague notion causes a certain uneasiness and, by reaction, a certain need for self-reassurance.

This is where compensation intervenes. Rather than begin the self-questioning, or self-admission or, above all, the self-reformation that would have to follow, we compensate, that is, we invoke or proclaim some value or exigency all the more loudly as we feel resentment against ourselves for not corresponding to this value or exigency.

The most frequent religious form of compensation consists in invoking the search for God to be better able to dissimulate one's flight from the truth. How many so-called religious vocations (above all, those calling themselves contemplative vocations) are simply flights from the truth about making oneself glamorous by the appearance of an alleged search for God.

Conclusions: We must accept ourselves in the truth of our being. The findings of psychologists on the subject of compensation rejoin the age old teachings of the spiritual writers on our fear of self-knowledge and our spontaneous flight whenever the opportunity exists to recognize the truth about ourselves.

Psychologists and spiritual writers also rejoin here the experience of Israel. The Hebrew people expressing its hatred for the wilderness in recriminations against its own leader, Moses, is the perfect image of man (individual or group) expressing through his attitudes and judgments about others his hatred of the emptiness he suspects in himself. "It is easier to hate oneself than one thinks."

"Francis," Christ is alleged to have said to him in the first months of his conversion, "learn to despise thyself if thou dost wish to know me." Francis of Assisi understood and practiced this lesson. He made a precept of it for his brothers in the second chapter of his rule. After having exhorted them never to judge or despise anyone he recommends," rather let each one judge and despise himself."

That is what it means to allow oneself to be led into the wilderness. It is to accept self-discovery willingly and in advance and to welcome ourselves in truth, even if this means welcoming ourselves as uninhabitable, sterile, and naked. Let us lend ourselves to this march through life prepared for us by God.

FIRST REFLECTION ON THE THEME
Into the Wilderness

A. Points for Meditation

1. This man rants away about universal selfishness. He is in reality ventilating his unconscious bitterness against himself. He is poisoning himself with his own selfishness.

2. This man glories in being tough, a "diehard," a knight errant and vindicator of wrongs in face of all authorities. An eternal adolescent, he is actually resentful of himself, for he has not yet overcome as a man the difficulties of passing from the necessary dependencies of childhood to the arduous autonomy of adulthood.

3. Here is a busy and preoccupied man. You have hardly met him when he is already glancing at his watch. If you knew him better you would discover an individual who is limited in his capacities and who has never recognized nor accepted nor loved his own true dimensions, that is, his own limits. He is in a "hurry," thus giving himself the illusion that he is playing an important part in the general life of society.

4. Another creates much ado over good companionship within a

small circle of intimates. It shows his refusal to recognize that, in fact, he is not very sociable.

5. Progressivism and juridicism are often only expressions of a lack of courage to assume the real present. A flight into the future allows one to escape with all the honors of war from the terrible day-to-day combat of life. Integrism and juridicism signify nothing better. Lacking real courage, one reassures oneself by affirming before others (and often only for others) the sacredness of some principle.

6. How many men extol dialogue when those near to them know how difficult it is to be heard by them. To invoke dialogue is reassuring anyone who uses monologue. It attributes one's isolation to the incomprehension and lack of acceptance by others.

7. Many men have made themselves the champions of freedom the better to justify before the inner eye of their conscience the authoritarianism with which they rule their own worlds.

8. The refusal to assume the responsibility for a situation is often an exacerbated form of the will to dominate.

9. People frequently avail themselves of the words heard from a spiritual director who has never seen them in their every day life to refuse the truth administered to them daily by the reactions of those with whom they live.

"THERE I WILL SPEAK TENDERLY TO HER" (Hos. 2, 16).

God leads man into the wilderness with a precise intention in mind, namely, that of stripping him of every artificiality and of freeing his *heart* so that it may hear the divine word. "There I will speak to his heart." The impersonator gives way to the person. God can then undertake the formation in depth of his human being and initiate it into his divine life.

Israel received its education from the Lord in the wilderness of Sinai. The people that God was to introduce into the promised land had to be formed from the crowd of slaves delivered out of Egypt. In the wilderness of our own lives here on earth, the Lord educates the true Israel that we are. The pack of slaves torn from sin by baptism must now learn here below to live as God's People. "For you are a people holy to the Lord your God; the Lord your God has chosen you to be a people for his own possession, out of all the peoples that are on the face of the earth" (Deut. 7, 6).

Let us therefore apply to ourselves the warnings addressed by the Lord to Israel in chapters 7, 8, and 9 of Deuteronomy.

A. Not to believe in one's own importance. In a first warning (chapter 7), the Lord calls on Israel to guard itself against the illusion of believing in its own importance.

Man is made in such a way that he needs to feel himself esteemed. But this legitimate need for the approval of others is corrupted when it becomes the need to be important. Instead of acting authentically, one becomes the prisoner of his own self-importance, of what he wishes to acquire. Thus, his entire conduct becomes deformed just as reality is deformed when it is viewed through an irregular pane of glass.

Chosen by God to receive the promised land, Israel was tempted by this very choice to exaggerate its own importance. God warned: "It was not because you were more in number than any other people that the Lord set his love upon you and chose you for you were

31

the fewest of all peoples, but it is because the Lord loves you . . ." (Deut. 7, 7-8).

To be baptized, to be a practicing Catholic, to be actively engaged in the apostolate, to belong to a religious family (above all if one is a cleric) has its risks. Illusions about oneself become more difficult to detect when they can more readily be clothed with the convenient glamor of divine rights.

To make oneself indispensable, to make another pay in dues of esteem the services that he needs, to boast of never giving way in the matter of recognized or acquired rights, to take advantage of the dignity and titles of a function even when that function is not exercised—all these are ways of behavior that are often evident in religious circles.

It sometimes happens that they are all the more frequent in certain individuals as their state of life places them more closely in the direct service of God. The authority that they hold becomes a veritable idol, that of their own personalities, which they impose on the adoration of others. It is reminiscent of Shakespeare's *Much Ado about Nothing.*

If a Christian cleric or layman wishes to allow baptismal grace to possess him, he must enter the wilderness of his own importance.

Whoever is preoccupied by the importance that others give to him refuses to enter this wilderness. The same is true of the man who, forgetful of true values, is less preoccupied by the common good than by the honorable mention with which he can begin his retirement. It is much the same with whoever imagines that *God* has called him on account of his qualities or his origin, or for his ideas or degrees, or on account of his prestige or his capabilities for influence. It is not for our own importance or because we might be of some advantage to him in establishing his kingdom that God has attached himself to us but only because in the interplay of events that initiated our existence, he has given us in advance a great measure of love.

B. Not to believe in our own "virtues." The second warning given by God to his people is to guard Israel against the illusion of expecting that the conquest of the promised land will be due to its exceptional military valor.

The practice of religion necessarily places the Christian apart from the commonplace. In everything that pertains to the faithful practice of his religion as well as whatever concerns an upright life, the Christian, in principle, must bear a living testimony that makes him different from others (cf. 1 Pet. 4, 1-7). Now from that to considering oneself better than others is but a step, and it is quickly taken. We come to believe in our own virtue.

Thus, the easy conquest of the promised land, the work of the power of the Lord, led Israel to believe itself more invincible than other peoples. Israel is warned against the illusions that can be occasioned by the exceptional aid it has received from God.

"Beware lest you say in your heart, 'my power and the might of my hand have gotten me this wealth.' You shall remember the Lord your God for it is he who gives you power to get wealth that he may confirm his covenant which he swore to your fathers . . ." (Deut. 8, 17.18).

The Christian of the twentieth century—at least in Europe—is acquainted with a type of life that he has inherited from previous generations. Centuries of fidelity to the commandments of God, and the mysterious efficacy of the Word of God and of the sacraments of Christ lie behind him.

The Christian of the Middle Ages was more aware than we are of the hereditary resurgence of barbarian characteristics. He was less astonished than we by human weakness and knew better than we do how to recognize himself both as the sinner and the saved.

We, on the contrary, because we have received a ready-made style of life representing an ideal of virtue, are inclined to equate this ideal of virtue with own persons. The prestige of a reputation to be upheld becomes the chief motivation for our actions. The fear of dishonor or of scandal is of more weight than the refusal of evil. Thus, the holy Catholic religion has been able to appear to many a Protestant and unbeliever as a school of hypocrisy.

If we set aside exaggerations and injustices, we must still recognize the excessive hold exercised on our religious behavior by an ideal of virtue such as purity and integrity, whose appearance for others, even at the cost of the truth, must be kept intact. How many "edifying" lies have thus been uttered by religious people! How many situations exist where the preponderance of the conventional has reduced to nothing the imperatives of reality and true charity!

Real virtue is quick to disappear when people make unwarranted

claims about it. This pretension is as favorable to the growth of phari-
saism in the Christian life as the contempt for the pagans was favorable to its growth in the history of the people of God. In fact, from
the people of God came forth the type of man immortalized by
Jesus in the parable of the publican and the pharisee.

We must accept the wilderness of our own virtues. We have
nothing of our own, neither from the social environment to which
we belong, nor from our own personal nature, that can pretend to
justify the call we have received. Human nature in us did not offer
a better soil than it did in others for the flowering of divine life. "God
called us with a holy calling not because of our own works but because
of his own purpose" (2 Tim. 1, 9).

C. Not to believe in our own   A last warning is to guard
   merits.   Israel against thinking of the con-
                                     quest of the promised land as a
                                     reward for its merits.

Even after accepting the wilderness of his own importance and
the wilderness of his own virtues, the Christian is still exposed to
illusions about himself. He can still believe in his own merits. He
may agree that no one is really any better than anyone else and in
the same breath tell you that if someone has accomplished things
others have not, then this should be taken into account.

Israel tended to believe that the possession of the promised
land was the reward of conduct pleasing to the Lord. "Do not say
in your heart, after the Lord your God has thrust them (the peoples)
out before you, 'It is because of my righteousness that the Lord has
brought me to possess this land'; know, therefore, that the Lord
your God is not giving you this good land to possess because of your
righteousness: for you are a stubborn people" (Deut. 9, 4-6).

In many of its prayers, the Church says that God in crowning the
merits of his saints is, in fact, crowning his own gifts. To those who
have done their duty thoroughly, Christ recommends the words "We
are unworthy servants" (Lk. 17, 10). Christ's invitation would be
a request to lie were it only concerned with the adoption of a formula.

Far from wishing to give us in these words nothing more than a
simple formula, Jesus invites us to establish the conviction in ourselves that what we give to God will never entitle us to any claim
upon him. We never do anything except through the dynamism which

he himself assures us flows in us moment by moment (cf. Prayer of the 12th Sunday after Pentecost).

A comic author once portrayed a monk adding up the minutes he had spent in prayer that surpassed those spent by his brother monks. Beyond this facile charge, there remains the fact that legions of Christians, clerics as well as laymen, *do* add up their claims; for services rendered to the Church, to Church institutions, to good works of the Church, and to churchmen. And if one does not go so far as to consider oneself a hero or a victim because of the work load one has assumed, he will at least attribute to himself a few certificates of merit, comparing what he has done with that which is left undone by so many others.

We must rid ourselves of these pretentions with which religious practice so easily encumbers our mentality as Christians. To attribute to ourselves rights and to believe in our own merits is to deceive ourselves (cf. Gal. 6, 3). We are thus refusing to enter the wilderness.

God pushes us along towards this wilderness of our merits leading us through the interplay of life, just as he leads us toward the wilderness of our own importance and virtues.

CONCLUSIONS

Let us not be astonished if we find that everything in us seems to find this void repugnant.

The need for security brings us back constantly to dreams of merit, importance, and virtue as was the case for Israel according to the flesh in the times of Christ.

"We are descendants of Abraham," they said proudly to Jesus, "and have never been in bondage to anyone" (Jn. 8, 33). Speaking of the people they said: "This crowd, who do not know the law, are accursed" (Jn. 7, 49).

The Temple, the Law, the purity of the race—these were the works through which Israel expressed its fidelity to the Alliance. It thus thought that it made of its God a god who received more honor and better service than all the other gods of neighboring lands. Nonetheless, several centuries had gone by since Jeremiah had summoned Israel not to place its confidence in the possession of the Temple

(Jer. 7, 4), but to desire a law written by God himself in the inner-most heart (Jer. 31, 33; 3, 14-18) and to practice true circumcision, that of the heart (Jer. 4, 4). But Israel according to the flesh clung to its own fidelities.

We, too, in spite of the numerous calls which life has allowed us to hear, cling to the visible manifestations of our fidelity to the Lord.

We obtain, if necessary by making ourselves ill (ulcers, manias, depressions), the recognition and acceptance by others of the validity of the ideas we cherish. We speak of acquired rights, unalterable certitudes, unassailable positions, and irreversible directions. What attachment to self such words cover!

In the parable of the prodigal son, the unfortunate son "came to himself" on that day when the artificial props of the somebody whose characteristics he had dreamed of fulfilling collapsed. Money, joyous companions, bread itself, he has not. Then he finds himself. Once again he is a "son" (Lk. 15, 14. 17).

It is so that we may be able to find ourselves, become "sons" once again, that God through the interplay of life's events procures in us and around us the collapse of our props.

In his fifth admonition, Francis of Assisi addresses himself to man. After enumerating all those things in which man can take satisfaction in himself, including the highest gifts, he says to him, "All these things are hurtful to you. . . ."

So that our riches may not be fatal to us, God leads us into the wilderness. At the end of the trial he will say to us as he said to Israel: ". . . You shall remember all the way which the Lord your God has led you these forty years in the wilderness . . . Know then in your heart that, as a man disciplines his son, the Lord your God disciplines you . . . that he might humble you and test you, to do you good in the end" (Deut. 8, 2.5.16).

It remains for us not to try to escape the interplay of existence in which God works to make our future happy, the eternal future of a child of God.

SECOND REFLECTION ON THE THEME
Into the Wilderness

A. POINTS FOR MEDITATION

1. First of all let us convince ourselves that it is hard for man to see himself. It is too bitter.

2. Clarity of vision regarding self is only possible on the condition that we rid ourself of the poison of excessiveness. It is necessary to know that in each man is acted out the drama lived by Adam. "You shall be as gods." The greatest wisdom is to accept oneself as a fact.

3. The appeal to the supernatural in the interpretation of real life situations must be regarded in advance as all the more ambiguous as the solutions it allows us to bring into action are proven to be easy ones. God has not gifted us with his grace to furnish us with alibis.

4. The apostle Paul tells his correspondents that he has counted as loss whatever gain he had from those things in which he had formerly placed his confidence and glory (cf. Phil. 3, 4.10). For us as for him the disavowal of all that is only appearance will give us access to reality. What are the appearances whose disavowal will allow me to accede to reality?

B. PARTICULAR THEMES

Priests and religious. Who would dare affirm that were he married, he would have lived his love perfectly in true conjugal chastity?

Theologians and preachers. What theoretician of social justice will dare assert that his conduct, had he been the manager of an enterprise, would have corresponded to the principles that are the object of his teaching?

Laymen. What union member can guarantee that were he the boss, he would have the same passion for justice that he has at present? What working man can claim that if he were born wealthy he would have his present understanding of fraternal solidarity? What boss can say that his point of view on the management of the plant would be the same if he were the worker?

C. TEXTS FOR READING AND PRAYER

a. Biblical Texts

Job 42, 1-7. Man collapses face to face with God.

Is. 5, 1-25. The "Wild grape vine" and the man who is satisfied with himself.

Jer. 7, 1-15. Emptiness of religious "practices" without respect for natural values.

Ezek. 12, 1-21. God creates emptiness around the man who will not do it for himself.

Phil. 3, 4-8. Paul creates his wilderness by stripping himself of all titles.

Lk. 15, 14-17. The prodigal enters into himself when a "wilderness" is created all around him.

b. Books

St. Francis, *Admonitions.*

c. Prayers

Is. 63, 15—64, 2. "Emptiness" in the absence of God.

Ps. 80. Outside of God creativity is not possible.

Ps. 69, 1-18. God is a help to him who implores him. The enemies are those parts of ourselves that lead us away from God.

Ps. 55. Call to God for help against the obscure forces of sin that disintegrate us in the innermost depths of our being.

Ps. 51. Confession of our sinful condition and confident appeal.

Final Theme

Jn. 3, 20-21.

III

In the Hands of God

> "The Lord himself led me amongst them (the lepers) and I showed mercy to them. And when I left them, that which had seemed to me bitter was changed for me into sweetness for body and soul."
>
> St. Francis of Assisi, *Testament*

"THOU HAST RUN IN ALL DIRECTIONS . . ." (Jer. 3, 13)

A. Solicitude of the Lord to allow man to express himself freely.

Fear and apprehension characterize the attitude of men in their relationship with God.

This instinctive reaction originates in the fact of every man's discovering himself to be naked when he is face to face with God. "I was afraid because I was naked." It is aggravated by the fact that God remains necessarily the mysterious stranger for man here on earth. When he approaches us, we ask fearfully, "What is he going to do to me?" or "What is he going to do with me?"

These are normal reactions, especially when God through the interplay of life causes the collapse around us of all the securities we have prepared for ourselves—our importance, our virtues, our merits. It is better at that time to admit our fear rather than to pretend we are spiritually brave. Above all, it is best to take advantage of these reactions of fear and defense to know ourselves better by meditating on God's conduct toward us.

God, in effect, knows us better than we can ever know ourselves. His conduct toward us is commanded by what he knows of us. He hopes to capture us as he has reason to hope that he can do.

In the history of humanity, we see God accepting the offerings of Abel. In a like manner, he has accepted all forms of cult elaborated

39

by men in all places and in all religions, provided that these manifestations were the expression of man's heart.

In the history of Israel, we see God accepting the cult that was rendered to him in the temple. A God of truth, he accepted as agreeable to himself even from his own chosen people, a liturgy whose display was often like that of a "sacred butchery" (cf. 2 Chron. 7, 5). He was only interested in whether this liturgy was really the expression of the heart of his people.

In the history of humanity as well as in the story of Israel we find this same patience of God (cf. 2 Pet. 3, 9). By this patience, God helped man to come out little by little from the hiding places where he had buried himself ever since he had sinned. He allowed man the full possibility to express himself freely. Far from reproaching him with his awkwardness and his imperfections, God encouraged him by accepting as a father every sincere expression which man either through religious cult or moral life managed to give of himself.

The same relationship between God and man is found on the level of our own personal lives. When we enter into life God, the better to dispel our fears, allows us every possibility to express ourselves freely in our relations with him. He places himself, in a way, on the level of our ideas, our tastes, even our weaknesses. He accepts our works. He sees in them the expression of our being that is seeking itself. Thus, a father and mother will accept the drawings and clay modelings of a child, however clumsy they may be, because the different traits of the child's personality are expressed gropingly through them.

But the inclination of our sinful nature quickly leads us to become infatuated with our own works. Just as the pagans were complacent about the cults of their own invention, and just as Israel admired itself in the splendors of the Temple and its ceremonies, so does each man admire himself and feel satisfied by that in which he excels. This one will exalt himself in the practice of some virtue, another will be satisfied with his activities of service or mutual help, and still another with his apostolate. We reply to God and the free gift of his love by playing the part of the diehard, the competent, the useful, or the devoted man.

We ignore, of course, the fact that in all of these works we are worshiping ourselves. But God who watches jealously over our being disposes the interplay of events so as to tear us away from this sin (cf. 1 Jn. 5, 21): "the idols"!

B. The purification of our aspirations beyond the collapse of our dreams.

The history of Israel foreshadows exactly the details of this solicitude of God for us.

When we read the sacred books that are marked more strongly by the influence of the priests (cf. the two Books of Chronicles) we become aware to what degree the cult rendered to God by his people had become their glory.

Descriptions of ceremonies, inventories of offerings presented to the treasury of the Temple, genealogies that guarantee the legitimacy of the "parts" to be played, statistics of the sacrificial victims (veritable statistics of a slaughter house)—all this shows us manifestly that Israel was in the process of becoming immersed in satisfaction with its own success as the People of God. It had made its God the highest honored and the best fed of all the divinities of the nations in that time.

Now comes the schism, the loss of national independence, the fall of Jerusalem and finally the ruin and destruction of the Temple. Everything in which Israel had found satisfaction is annihilated.

Lesser trials would not have sufficed to tear Israel away from the cult of an expression of itself which was becoming a real idol!

Every Christian, a true Israel, must become conscious of the need to be torn away from the cult of self-expression when it takes on this character of idolatry. The second chapter of the Book of Hosea can help us understand the wide range of this self-awareness: "And she did not know that it was I who gave her the grain, the wine and the oil, and who lavished upon her silver and gold which they used for Baal" (Hos. 2, 8). Nourished with the bread of the Word and with the eucharist, cleansed and refreshed with the precious wine that is the blood of the Lord, strengthened with the divine chrism of baptism and confirmation, the Christian can become an idolator and adore the image he has made of himself out of the gifts the Lord has lavished upon him.

"O that you had hearkened to my commandments. Then your peace would have been like a river, and your righteousness like the waves of the sea. Your offspring would have been like the sand" (Is. 48, 18). Happiness and holiness, a lasting fruitfulness, are impossible for the man who wants to be his own rule of judgment and conduct, the center of thought and action. This man erects Baals with the gifts he received from God (cf. Ezek. 15, 9. 20).

Therefore, it is not surprising that God then allows everything in which we have taken satisfaction to come to ruin.

And here is a man who after having exhausted himself at playing the angel wakes up one day to find he is playing the beast. And another who has worn himself out converting others comes to ask himself one day if he himself has faith. Still another who was so proud of the integrity of his actions catches himself one day participating in a racket or sees doubt cast upon his work.

Perhaps they will reproach God in their prayers for not having furthered their efforts. "Did they not have in view his glory alone?" Each one of them learns thus from the Lord that he was working only for the glory of his own self-expression for which the service of God or of men was merely the occasion or pretext.

It is useless, then, to pray or entreat the Lord to fulfill our dreams of sanctity or even of a fruitful apostolate. Far from intervening to bring about for us the success to "justify" us (the victory over a temptation, for example), God will not prevent errors, failures, or even falls in the course of our existence.

"I have forsaken my house, I have abandoned my heritage, I have given the beloved of my soul into the hands of her enemies" (Jer. 12, 7).

It could then happen that we would persist in the resolves to accomplish our dreams, the service of God or of some great cause in which only our own glory was expressed.

Our attitude in this would be a repetition of the attitude of the Jews who were stubbornly determined with Nehemiah to rebuild the Temple (cf. Neh. 12; Ezra 5 and 6) and who took the most rigorous measures to assure the purity of the race and watched over the application of the precepts of the law (cf. Ezra 9; 2 Chron. 24; Neh. 8).

To accomplish our purpose better we may accept or even ask some help from the "enemy," and make some unavowed compromise with our consciences. The Jews even went so far as to accept the help of Herod, the hated Idumean. But in all this, God's help will be lacking to us or, more exactly, aid will be given to us to help us recognize our limits, although this might result in making us fall the harder. "Why wish to die?" asks the Lord (Ezra 18, 21). "Thou hast run in all directions with strangers," said the Lord to Israel, "and thou hast not heard my voice" (Jer. 3, 13).

Let us not therefore be surprised if we have to become acquainted with the crushing experience of inner defeat. It could even occur that, thinking of our dreams of holiness and fulfillment, we feel we are walking over a field of ruins within ourselves. "The shameful thing has devoured all that for which our fathers labored" (Jer. 3, 24).

Frustrated expectations, destroyed hopes, useless efforts, fruitless works . . . This annihilation can be the most decisive step forward we can take in our existence, for in it, we discover the value of the cries that rise to God from a contrite heart. "A contrite heart, O God, thou wilt not despise" (Ps. 51, 19).

C. Consciousness of the emptiness of self and conversion to the Lord.

For Israel it was the bitterness of the nation's trials that formed the abyss wherein it awoke to the consciousness of the need to purify its relations with God.

Each Christian arrives at this same consciousness when he begins to experience the emptiness of an existence spent entirely in the satisfaction of futilities. He then knows the state of discontent to which our nature is necessarily condemned when the Lord abandons his house and leaves that which he cherished in the hands of his enemies.

It is somewhat rare to see this awareness attain real depth before a man has reached the age of forty. This is the age of the second birth. Man then sees the eldest of his own children stand before him and choose his own destiny. It matters little if this eldest son happens to be a flesh and blood human being or a cherished work, an idea or a long pursued and well beloved project. Faced with his eldest son, man becomes conscious of the practical idolatry in which he has been living. Every possibility of encounter with the true God depends on this consciousness.

This probably will never happen. Thus, the self-satisfied go through life convinced that they have never erred nor fallen. They have foreseen everything, have arranged everything for the best, and cannot recall an error or a failure. They have nothing but admiration for themselves and their own works. "Beatifically unconscious" their self-made idols will remain enthroned in the sanctuary of their inner worlds until their last hours. Nothing can make these men as dangerous as investing them with authority by giving them some responsibility in the ecclesiastical order. They can then reign in the midst of a world of spiritual suffering while serenely ignoring the dramas that are being lived on account of them.

It might happen that this consciousness will be refused. This is the case of the "malcontents" unsatisfied with everything. Their philosophy is condensed in a few favorite expressions of the following sort: "We have understood." "We know what you are trying to do." The blasés and the disillusioned who speak this way have not understood anything. It remains for them to understand the essential fact that they have been disappointed only by the idol they have made of themselves.

Being self-satisfied and dissatisfied with everything represents two extremes. In between is the mass of those who with Israel call upon the Lord.

"All our pleasant places have become ruins. Wilt thou restrain thyself at these things, O Lord? Wilt thou keep silent and afflict us sorely?" (Is. 63, 13; cf. also Is. 63, 14—64, 12).

These are those who have been led into the wilderness and have known hunger, thirst, and fear. But they discover that the reactions of their hapless human nature far from being chastisements are remedies. Hunger, thirst, and fear are calls from God to us through our own human nature. At the same time they are cries from that nature to God: "For the Lord has created a new thing on the earth: a woman protects a man" (Jer. 31, 22).

The wonder of the Lord's action throughout the course of history as well as in the secret of each human heart is this: God creates a new heart (cf. Ps. 51, 12), and man who in his self-satisfaction turned away from God will begin anew to seek God of his own will, out of his own undeniable need.

"And in that day, says the Lord, you will call me 'my husband' and no longer will you call me 'my Baal' " (Hos. 2, 16).

Conclusions: Learn to find the   All the vicissitudes of human
Lord in all the trials of exist-   existence find their explanation in
ence.   the confession to which they lead
                                        our nature: "I will return to my
first love." In all these vicissitudes, God was present (cf. Is. 48, 17).
He prepared the perfect accord between the aspirations of our nature
and the solicitations of his grace.

It is therefore of capital importance to situate ourselves in every
given circumstance within the plan that God is pursuing. It is even
more important to do this when we are burdened with error,
weakness, and sin. The systems of Christian perfection that we have
in our minds become prejudicial to us when we forget that weakness,
error, and sin are an integral part of God's plan for us.

In the 17th chapter of his first Rule, Francis of Assisi invites his
brothers not to be complacent in any of their successes. "We ought
rather to rejoice when we fall into divers temptations, and when we
bear some afflictions or sorrows." Indeed these situations tear us
away from pride and vainglory. They save us from the worst danger
of all: the danger of shutting ourselves in, of drying up, of dying in
the cult of some expression of our own self.

"If you return, O Israel, says the Lord, to me you should return. If
you remove your abominations from my presence and do not waver"
(Jer. 4, 1).

We would not have to flee from God anymore if we would rid ourselves of our "abominations" (our idols), that is, if we would renounce every image of ourselves (pride and vainglory), and would
love our beings as we have received them from the Lord.

FIRST REFLECTION ON THE THEME
In the Hands of God

A. POINTS FOR MEDITATION

1. To refuse the lessons of life because we have not found in them
the accomplishment of the dreams with which we have deluded our-

selves is to make any true spiritual life impossible for us. We are fleeing from God, the master of circumstances, even if in this flight we persuade ourselves that we have sought and found the Lord.

2. When a Christian aspires to perfection, he strongly risks placing himself at the service of an image of himself. In the practical realization of this image he will not have long to wait before he encounters a thousand obstacles. Instead of being discouraged, he can learn to discern in these obstacles the instruments to purify his dream. Gradually, he will be delivered from the search for his own perfection and will begin to desire the perfection of the life of God in himself as well as in other men.

3. It so happens that men wishing to serve other men devote themselves to the promotion of an ideal. The passion with which they give themselves to this promotion exposes them, one day, to place this ideal above the men whose good it was supposed to serve. The opposition or resistance encountered, then, of others are valuable and whoever is not offended by them can find there a light on the limits and perhaps on the narrowness of his own views and choices. If he can accept the implications of this, he will come away more apt to serve with greater purity of intention the ideal with which he has become infatuated. This ideal will remain at the service of the real condition of man.

4. When a Christian wants to serve the Church, he spontaneously devotes himself to gain acceptance for the image of the Church which is personally dear to him. He can, without knowing it, be only at the service of his own inner constructions. Fortunately he will meet resistance and opposition! This resistance and opposition far from making him renounce the service of the Church can be for him the occasion to enter into a real service of the Church. This real service of the Church will take into consideration at the same time both the fulfillment of the personality of the Christian and the respect of the human reality in the midst of which he lives.

5. There are men who cannot console themselves for having failed or been unsuccessful. They are more sensitive to the humiliation suffered by their idol than to the solicitude with which the true God is pursuing them.

6. "My purity . . . my chastity. . . ." What equivocal expressions! Purity and chastity are then only expressions of vanity. No one

is pure or chaste "outside of the Lord." If a person wants to be pure and chaste because of the halo to be achieved, he may find that the halo must be purchased by wounds that are far more deadly than the pitiful wounds of the flesh.

"BEHOLD I HAVE GRAVEN YOU
ON THE PALMS OF MY HANDS . . ." (Is. 49, 16).

A. A foreshadowing of the love with which God loves us is given to us in the love with which God loved his people Israel.

Listening in to our own personal lives heard as a true word of God reveals us to ourselves and disposes us to confess, "Confiteor . . . I recognize . . ."

But at the same time this attentive listening is a revelation to us of the love with which God loves us. In everything that is given to us to live, we discover that God has always been a Father to us.

St. John recalls with insistence that God loved us first (cf. 1 Jn. 4, 10)

God is first in the love with which he loves us with absolute priority. It is not a simple chronological priority. It is ontological. The love with which he loves us is the very reason for our coming into existence. This is why the love with which God has loved us is a love without repentance. "I have loved you with an everlasting love . . ." (Jer. 31, 3; cf. also 2, 1). The love with which God loves us goes therefore to the real being God creates in us, whatever the ups and downs inflicted on this being by our errors and weaknesses. As long as this being pursues its becoming in the night here below, God continues to love and to watch over it.

The relations of God with his people, Israel, are the perfect foreshadowings of this attention God bestows on the being he gives us.

This loving attention is manifested first of all in the fact that God never regrets having called Israel to be his people.

Of course, there are incidents (cf. Num. 14, 10ff.) where sentiments of having suffered betrayal and projects of destruction are attributed to God. But in actual fact, when the time of action arrives, the heart of God does not follow his plan.

"How can I give you up, O Ephraim! How can I hand you over, O Israel! My heart recoils within me, my compassion grows warm and tender. I will not execute my fierce anger, I will not destroy

48

Ephraim; for I am God and not man, . . . and I will not come to destroy" (Hos. 11, 7-9).

Isaiah in chapter 54 describes the same situation. God cannot contemplate ceasing to love his people: " 'For a brief moment I forsook you, but with great compassion I will gather you. In overflowing wrath for a moment I hid my face from you but with everlasting love I will have compassion on you . . . For the mountains may depart and the hills be removed, but my steadfast love shall not depart from you, and my covenant of peace shall not be removed, says the Lord who has compassion on you' " (Is. 54, 7.8.10). God himself seems astonished that his love for his people should have such power over his heart.

"Is Ephraim my dear son? Is he my darling child? For as often as I speak against him, I do remember him still. Therefore my heart yearns for him. I will surely have mercy on him, says the Lord" (Jer. 31, 20).

All Scripture witnesses to the fact that the love of God for us is freely bestowed.

God loves his people because he is God. He knows neither our disenchantments nor our bitter rancors (cf. Jer. 3, 12-13). He is only tenderness and pity (cf. Ps. 103 and the Book of Jonah). His love is from all time (cf. Ps. 136).

Now this love of God for Israel throughout the vicissitudes of its history is the figure of the love which God bears for each one of us, true Israels of God. This love is not therefore a simple disposition of good will, a sentiment of God in regard to us, an attitude adopted by him on account of some interesting feature he has been able to see in us, his creatures.

His love is his divine will in which his divine nature is expressed. And this nature is love. It is an involvement of all of himself— Father, Son, and Holy Spirit—that makes him present and active in all of our lives. Just as he was in the midst of his people, he is in the midst of each one of us at the very point where the dynamism of our being springs forth, in that mysterious center from which proceeds all that, in truth, we are.

"I am . . . the Holy One in the midst" (cf. Deut. 7, 21 and Hos. 11, 9). Present and acting in us, he heals even those wounds which by our past resistances we have inflicted upon ourselves. "Your hurt is incurable and your wound is grievous . . . because your sins are flagrant . . . I will restore health to you and your wounds I will heal, says the Lord" (Jer. 30, 12. 14. 17).

There is no question of ever having failed. It is simply a question of believing that in all the situations we are given to live, and even in the worst of the disillusions that wound us, the Lord has always held us in his hand: "Behold, he says to our disabled being, Behold, I have graven you on the palms of my hands!" (Is. 49, 16). It is for us to establish ourselves inside this love with which God loves us in such a way as to place our being in the best position for the expression of itself.

B. To love oneself with the love with which God loves us and for this to deny oneself pessimism and satisfaction in suffering, and to learn to accept help from others.

We will not really be able to hear expressed fully and in all its truth that word of God which is for each one of us our own nature if we do not love ourselves enough to allow that nature to express itself.

Of course we need less to learn to love ourselves than to learn to love ourselves the right way. How can we love ourselves rightly? We have the example in Israel of those who believed in the Lord despite all trials. We will love ourselves rightly by never doubting the love of God for us (cf. Ps. 130). However dark the night of our errors and faults, like Israel, we wait on the Lord. This demands of us very specially that we never become lost in discouragement or disillusionment about ourselves. There must be no pessimism, no satisfaction in suffering, and no refusal of help from others.

Pessimism can be explained by poor liver function. This justified assertion can show us the relativity of the judgments that we may happen to proffer on life, on the world, and on ourselves.

The man who has become conscious of his limits, of his weakness, and of the disproportion between the dreams that he has cherished and the reality of which he is capable can be tempted by pessimism. Of what use are so many dreams of holiness leading in the end to a life that just drags along? What good are so many aspirations toward a better world when everyone stumbles on the same obstacles of indifference or ingratitude? "Holiness? It's not for me! Do something? It won't change anything."

To love oneself truly is to believe that until our last instant, God can bring forth from our being real holiness and fruitfulness. He who gives in to pessimism either ignores or then refuses grace and at the same time tramples on nature. His attitude willingly finds a justification for itself in the events that follow.

"You see, I told you so," he says. In reality, these events are, at least in part, the bitter fruit of the negative attitude in which the pessimist has locked himself.

As contrary to true love of oneself as pessimism is the attitude of taking satisfaction in suffering. "Suffering is necessary," becomes the final expression of an entire view of life. It is quite true that we must suffer, and the Christian through his baptism knows that he is destined to carry his cross with Christ. But he also knows that the sufferings by which the passion of Christ is continued in him are not those to which he should resign himself passively, lacking the courage to fight.

In welcoming and embracing the sufferings that life provides for him, the Christian never settles himself down into suffering nor into the settled opinion to do nothing to get out of it. To do nothing to improve one's situation or condition is to refuse to love oneself. The attitude that consists in being satisfied with suffering—and very often true in the pessimistic attitude as well—is an alibi that man gives himself. It is a disguised and seemingly honorable way of avoiding the most difficult form that love of self can assume—that of loving oneself enough to accept help from others.

As a general rule, it is really through a lack of true love of self that man will not allow himself to have recourse to this help and may even refuse it.

Christ accepted without difficulty the help Simon of Cyrene, because in his passion, he was not acting a part. (Cf. Mk. 15, 21.) When we refuse help from others, do we really know the meaning of our refusal? Perhaps the impersonator in us who wants to get along on his own and not to need others is once again the object of greater solicitude and attention than are the poor human persons we really are!

One sometimes meets individuals who complain bitterly that they have not found from those near to them (colleagues, companions, relatives, or neighbors) the help which they needed. It so happens that these individuals are often the same ones who through their attitudes have done everything within their power to make others understand that they needed no one. Perhaps they wanted above all to create this illusion for themselves.

To accept and, if necessary, even to seek out the help of others is surely one of the most difficult forms of true love of self.

In our own times this form of love of self will often consist in admitting that one is in need of medical and psychological aid. In the rhythm of an existence where the part of our being the most often pressed into service is the nervous system it is normal to find that this help is often indispensable.

Our contemporaries need to be told that one can be a saint while being subject to tendencies of anguish or of aggressivity or while being sensual or irritable. But one cannot be a saint while refusing to be helped by another to reabsorb one's anguish or one's aggression or to go beyond the reflexes of one's nature and to overcome one's temper. How can one tend toward holiness when one accepts inwardly the disintegration of the person created by God rather than to suffer the slightest injury to the impersonator, the creature of our ambitions, our illusions and our dreams? It is not thus that we love ourselves with the love with which God loves.

Conclusions: The "yes" of our being to God. To love ourselves with the love with which God loves is to say "Yes" without any reservations to the being that we receive from God. This Yes is finally a Yes to God, the *AMEN* of our being! (cf. 2 Cor. 1, 19-22).

Now, everything by which we have pity on our own infirmities is a part of this Yes that our being must give to God who creates and saves it. This Yes is the equivalent of recognizing God as our Father and blessing him for having created us. By this Yes, we embrace the totality of our being, that is, we embrace it burdened with sin, inasmuch as it is a leper.

"The Lord himself led me amongst them (the lepers) and I showed mercy to them. And when I left them, that which had seemed to me bitter was changed for me into sweetness of body and soul." Thus writes Francis of Assisi in his *Testament*.

It will have been enough if we practice mercy toward our being by accepting ourselves totally without refusing any of the things of which we may perhaps have an intimation, and be afraid to admit to ourselves. Because we will have embraced ourselves "insomuch as we are lepers," above all if this proceeding has implied the recourse to one or another of our brothers, we shall see all things changed for us into sweetness of body and soul. For this attitude puts in their rightful place the most essential elements of our own salvation. As in any attitude of acceptance of our own nature, we are in full accord with the will of God who loves us, who creates us and who calls us to live of his own life.

At the end of this course it will be possible for us to hear in truth the word of God that our own personal nature is for each one of us. At this point, in fact, this nature in us will be loved sufficiently and truly enough to have arrived at expressing, according to its real being, the being that it has from God.

This requires very particularly that we know how to be silent in the face of ourselves (before our dreams, aspirations, desires, and above all, envies of every kind). For the deep knowledge that a man can have of what he really is must be measured by the silence that he has the courage to keep in the presence of the manifestations and expressions of his being so as to arrive at placing himself in an attitude of attention to the word by which God continually creates him (cf. Ezek. 16, 62-63).

SECOND REFLECTION ON THE THEME
In the Hands of God

A. POINTS FOR MEDITATION

1. To believe, having experienced this truth in our lives, that the love of God is present simultaneously to all that we are and to all that we carry in ourselves, is the best preparation for the acceptance of self.

2. Neither success nor failure are guarantees in themselves to a man that he has let himself be led by God. But in success as in failure, man does not cease to be in the hands of God.

3. It is easily harmful for a man to recall his successes. To recall successes is not to nourish a man but to puff him up.

4. It will always be salutary to recall failure if we do so with confidence as if to a testimonial of the solicitude of our Father. Thus assumed, failure can always detach our being from some artifice. It brings us to our true dimensions by bursting the bubble of our bombast.

5. To know and to accept oneself never means to be resigned to what one is and to do nothing about it. On the contrary, the better we will have identified the basis from which our progress must be made, the more capable we will be of getting out of our present condition.

6. There is no knowledge of self without silence, and man needs courage to plunge himself into a silence which risks giving him true knowledge of himself.

7. The civilization of noise can be as prejudicial to man as a civilization of drugs.

8. Even the professionals of silence can lose the meaning of what silence represents in a human existence. From the need for silence in the outdoors that the working man can satisfy only during his brief holidays, the religious must learn again the vital character of the silence that is given to them the year round.

9. The sacrament of penance is not a washing or a cleansing; it is a guarantee that we are loved and embraced by a Father whatever our actions as sinners may have been.

10. We are dearer to God because of our weakness than through our virtues.

B. Texts for Reading and Prayer

a. Biblical Texts

The prophetic books are full of the promise of a renovation that God will work in us through the trials of existence.

Is. 51; 54; 55; 60; 62. The wonderful renewal that is promised to us.
Jer. 2; 3; 19ff. Calls of God.
Ezek. 34; 36; 37. God strikes but also he resurrects.

Job. The entire book. Reflect upon 4, 1-2.
Zech. 7; 8. Note especially Zech. 8, 15.
Rev. 31; 32. The end to which we are called.
Lk. 15, 20. The father was waiting, he had never doubted his son. It is up to the sons not to doubt the Father.

b. Books

Thomas of Celano. *Vita Prima.* Part I. chap. 7.
St. Francis. *Testament,* vv. 1-4.

c. Prayers

Bar. 1, 15—3, 9. Imploration to God who leads all.
Pss. 105; 106; 107. Miracles of God leading his people.
Pss. 38; 44. God, the only salvation in adversity.
Ps. 103. Immense tenderness of a God who is Father.
Ps. 136. Litany of thanksgiving. Each one can add to it his own personal reasons for chanting it. "For his steadfast love endures forever."

Final Theme

Is. 49, 16. ("I have graven you on the palms of my hands.")

PART ONE: CONCLUSIONS

The first word addressed by God to man is man's own nature. This is, in actual fact, marred by the burden of sin.

Meditating on the pages of the Old Testament allows us to find in the history of Israel our own personal histories as well as enlightenment on our acts and behavior. We can thus discern in our innermost being that which is word of God from that which is refusal of that word.

From this confession, which prepares us for sacramental confession, a better knowledge of ourselves becomes possible. This knowledge has as its aim the conformity of our actions with our being. Behavior and life are revised in the light of our true nature.

To take our true nature into account is: to aspire to fulfill that which is best in it, but to limit ourselves to that of which it is really capable; to accept our weaknesses without self-deception or bitterness, and to seek our progress without illusions or pretensions; finally, to expect all from the love with which God has freely loved us.

Thus will we be attentive to the first word of God, that wholly personal word addressed by God to each one of us and to all humanity collectively.

In this word is formulated, in a certain way, the conditions of my personal destiny and of the destiny of the human family.

PART TWO
Others

I

He Was Obedient
to His Fellowmen

> "He who would rather suffer persecution than wish
> to be separated from his brethren, truly abides in
> perfect obedience because he lays down his life
> for his brothers."
>
> Francis of Assisi, *Admonitions*, 3

"THE LORD HAS OPENED MY EAR" (Is. 50, 5).

A. One expression sums up the obedience of Christ: All through his life he was possessed of a willing ear. The Epistle to the Hebrews in chapter 10 quotes some verses from the 40th Psalm and places them on the lips of Christ as he enters this world.

"Sacrifice and oblation thou dost not desire but thou hast given me an open ear. Burnt offering and sin offering Thou hast not required. Then I said: 'Lo, I come; in the roll of the book it is written of me I delight to do thy will, O my God, thy law is within my heart' " (Ps. 40, 6-8).

By this declaration, Christ proclaims his will to obey. "I delight to do thy will, thy law is within my heart." At the same time we are told that this obedience has nothing in common with the celebration of a cult. "Sacrifice and offering thou dost not desire." There remains for us to understand the two expressions that form a sort of repetition: "Thou hast given me an open ear . . . Then I said: 'Lo, I come.' "

The reading of the Gospels (above all Matthew and John) sometimes gives the impression that Jesus in his life obeyed his Father by fulfilling point by point a plan established in advance. The knowledge that Jesus had of events that were to come contributes to this

59

impression, and the evangelists insist upon it to make evident the transcendence of the master.

But this manner of expression must not deceive us and the phrase, "thou hast given me an open ear," can help us to discover exactly what the obedience of Christ really was in its human reality. We will seek to understand the content of this expression apart from its symbolism (cf. Deut. 15, 16. with Is. 50, 5).

To have an open ear is to be capable of hearing, of listening; it is to be in a disposition of obedience. Here the Semitic expression rejoins Latin philosophy in which "to obey" derives from the composite "ob-audire," which means literally to "hold the ear open in the direction from which the voice is coming."

It can be said of Christ that when he entered this world, he declared himself to be "all ears."

It is for us to fathom how the Lord lived concretely in his daily existence the "open ear" attitude to which he lays claim here.

B. Situations lived by Jesus: In them he contributes to the common good. The different situations lived by Christ on earth have one thing in common in their diversity: in all these situations Christ is an intimate part of the milieu of his neighbors and contemporaries through the personal contribution he made to the common good.

In Nazareth after the time of his childhood when he lived near Joseph and Mary, Jesus worked for others. He earned his living from the price of his labor accomplished for others. Thus, he inserted himself on the level of Joseph's profession into the network of economic exchanges of his little town. These economic exchanges were modest, it is true, and of an elementary type, but they were nonetheless real. Jesus brought his own contribution to the common good of a locality (cf. Lk. 2, 51; Mk. 6, 3).

Around his thirtieth year the consciousness of his mission made it a duty for Jesus to leave the workshop and consecrate himself to announcing the Good News. Here again, it is the will to serve the common good that determines the conduct of Jesus. He brings to men something of far more value than a material contribution made of furniture and agricultural tools. He brings love, unity, peace, the

Kingdom. And he is so well aware of serving the common good that he claims for himself and his apostles the means to sustain a life consecrated to the greater good of everyone. "For the laborer deserves his wages" (Lk. 10, 7; Mt. 10, 10).

Here the conduct of Christ begins to arouse his adversaries, and he is threatened with death (cf. Jn. 5, 18). He could, of course, cease talking to men about his Father and their Father; he could simply return to the workshop to take up once more a calm and peaceful life near his mother, Mary. But to cease announcing the Good News would, in fact, be to betray men, his brothers. Their common good demands of Christ to persevere at whatever cost to himself in this mission (cf. Jn. 6, 37). So he perseveres even when this search for the common good of men ends, in final analysis, with his own overwhelming defeat.

Submitting himself unto the end to the common good of his brothers, he accepts this defeat, for it has become necessary so that the testimony that Christ had given by his words to the truth would not be annuled in the eyes of men by an evasion.

Such are the successive situations of Christ in Nazareth, of Christ announcing the Kingdom, of Christ in his passion. These situations allow us to discover in what the obedience of the Lord consisted. This obedience had been the acceptance of interhuman relations in the pursuit of the common good, even when this pursuit of the common good became for him a cause of suffering, of opposition, and of final defeat. The Son of God, because he is a son of man, accepts himself in the whole framework of his human nature. He keeps his ears open, continuing to pursue the common good which can be obtained only by making him a victim. This is his obedience. It is far more admirable than the submission he showed as a child to Joseph and Mary which could not have cost him very much.

C. Jesus is faithful to this common good through fidelity to the word of God that others are for him.

These reflections enlighten us. They show us where Christ's will to submit himself to the common good finally led him. He comes to admit, he who is the Word incarnate, that creatures, even sinful ones, can be for him as a man the mediators of the divine will. In the very measure that a crea-

ture had some part to play in the common good of society, Christ
knew himself and wished himself obedient to it. In the face of every
creature, he keeps a total awareness of his dignity as Son of God. St.
John gives us three instances of this in the 13th chapter of his Gospel (cf. Jn. 3, 13.19). But this full consciousness of his divine dignity never caused him to shirk from the servitudes that derived from
his belonging to human communities. He accepted himself as a
member of a family, an ethnic, a religious, and a political community. It is fidelity to the common good of these communities, of which
he is a member, that submits Christ to Joseph, Herod, Caiphas
and Pilate. In regard to these different communities, Christ keeps an
open ear when the fact of belonging to them on the religious and
political levels is a cause of suffering for him. He does not set himself apart from them. When these communities become, in the person of their rulers, hostile, unjust, and even fatal to him, he continues
to situate himself inside of them. He accepts himself as dependent
on them; he consents to a death that comes to him from them.

Christ, the Word of God, keeps himself attentive to that word
of God that other men are for him insofar as he himself is a man.
Because he is a man, he does not refuse to hear any of the calls that
come to him from men. He is attentive to them with an open ear;
he hears them and he responds to them. In his workshop at Nazareth,
while he busies himself with wood, Jesus hears the voices of his clients. Such and such a job must be completed or delivered on a certain day. But beyond these immediate calls, there are others he
already perceives, and they are more mysterious and more urgent
for his heart.

His Jewish brothers called to him through the ritualism in which
the cult of his Father was already becoming rigid. The Roman world
called to him through the vision of a peace that relied too much on
the force of arms. The world of slavery called to him by crushing
all those whom the hazards of existence had placed under the heels of
others. It is in answer to all these calls that Jesus left his workshop
to enter into the problems of men.

Thus, he revealed to men the real value of their world. This
world in its innermost reality is a world of the children of God, and
all the cries that rise from this world of men towards a man, even if

this man is the Word of God made flesh, must be listened to as the words of God.

This is the scope of the testimony rendered by Christ in his life passed in the service of the common good above all, when for it, he goes so far as to lose all that a divine Person could lose: his body and blood, his human life and honor.

Conclusions: The common good of men, a sacred reality. Of all the realities that have come to existence in the created universe, the human life of Jesus is certainly the most sacred that can be imagined or conceived.

Christ as man is the perfect finality to which all the effort of the universe had tended. Now, Christ makes his existence subject to the common good of men. He goes even further, for he sacrifices his life to their common good. We must conclude that the common good of men is an even more sacred reality than the earthly life of Jesus, the true Son of God (cf. 2 Cor. 5, 15—17, 16).

This one conclusion is enough to make us understand that the common good of men is a reality of a superior order. The common good of men cannot, first of all, be reduced to a society of law and order. Neither can it be limited to the simple well-being of all. Jesus did not die to maintain law and order or well being. He sacrificed his life to establish the true common good of a truly human order, the order of truth and love, which consists, first of all, in the gathering together of the children of God who are dispersed. He died to re-establish interhuman relations in their true significance. By making his life subject to every requirement contained in these interhuman relations, he makes us see in them the very preparation of the King-dom of God.

We learn from Christ that obedience is not a disposition wherein simple necessities of right or of fact are swallowed or submitted to. Obedience is a disposition in which are manifested the links that bind and subject one individual to another because they love one another.

"Let them (the brothers) . . . in the spirit of charity willingly serve and obey each other and this is the true and holy obedience of our Lord Jesus Christ," writes Francis of Assisi (Rule, 5).

It is from Christ that man learns to obey in the loving acceptance of the bonds that unite him to others. In the light of Christ the bonds of obedience take on their consistency, solidity, and true value in the consciousness that we have of placing ourselves at the service of a sacred common good. This common good is the opportunity given to all men to be men as fully as possible so that all of them will be able to enter the fullness of their dignity as children of God (cf. Eph. 4, 25—5, 22).

FIRST REFLECTION ON THE THEME
He Was Obedient to His Fellowmen

A. Points for Meditation

1. Here are some expressions whose content is worthy of evaluation when we are using them: "I made arrangements not to know it . . ." "I managed to get out of that one . . ." "I'm not that dumb . . ."

2. To follow Christ in his obedience is the very expression of our faith. We obey because we believe firmly that the course of events will prove us to have been right even if in the end, they do so only in the manner with which they proved Christ to be right in his resurrection (cf. 1 Cor. 15, 19.30.32).

3. In feudal times the obedience of Christ freed the weak from the tyranny of the strong who were better endowed physically. It accomplished the miracle of placing the strong at the service of the weak (chivalry). The obedience of Christ can deliver the weak from all the tyrannies exercised by all sorts of power holders (those who are better equipped financially, technically, geographically, juridically, numerically). Only the obedience of Christ can accomplish the miracle of placing these powers at the service of the weak.

4. One cannot associate legitimately in the same human being the curiosity to know and the firm resolution to disinterest oneself from information that will necessarily bring responsibility with it.

5. Modern man knows the real condition of the world, its development and its hunger. He will therefore be questioned by the Lord on his actual obedience to this world situation. The Christian can discern the importance of this connection.

6. To obey is to acquit oneself of dues. This makes one reflect on the ambiguity of the word "charity" when it is reduced to the meaning of liberality of the possessor.

7. For religious and those who are cloistered: Newspapers, radio, and television are means of knowledge. Their use is good and can even be excellent. Even so, knowledge must be translated into action. Should we desire a knowledge of which we well know in advance that it will not risk compromising us in action? To know and not to act leads to death. This is not obedience.

"BE SUBJECT TO ONE ANOTHER . . ." (Eph. 5, 21).

A. Christ brought a natural ideal of human solidarity to perfection, expressing it in his attitude of obedience.

"Thou hast given me an open ear." These words that Christ addressed to God, his Father, on entering this world can be addressed by every man to Christ since the passion.

Whether it concerns relations with his immediate neighbors inside of some restricted community or of broader relationships on the level of larger communities, man has learned from Christ the answer that he must give to all human situations. This answer is not a theory or a philosophical system; it is a situation that Christ chose and lived. It is the submission of one's whole being to the appeals that come to us from the communities to which we belong. The common good must be regarded as sacred.

Long before Christ, men had foreseen this reality of a sacred common good to which everything else had to be subordinated. But in the hesitations of their research, they had made sacred a common good limited to the one group they formed themselves which was often in opposition to other human groups which were regarded as dangerous or as enemies. Even today after two thousand years of Christianity, it suffices to touch certain chords in man's heart to awaken in him vestiges of a heredity gained in times when the common good was identified with the instinct of group conservation and when this conservation sometimes necessitated the destruction of other groups. But the situation lived voluntarily by Christ has opened man's ear. Man has been given to understand that fidelity to the common good of all men must be able to lead him to his own destruction without distinction of groups among men.

The individual comes to existence only through the human family to which he belongs, and he becomes a human person only within the network of relations assured him by the human communities of different types to which in some way or another he is attached. This

66

dual and necessary dependence brings with itself for each human being a *necessary condition of obedience.*

Christ opened man's ears by revealing to him through his example that this necessary condition of obedience cannot be reduced to a simple condition of passive subjection. It cannot be only the acceptance of a right or a fact. From Christ man learns that true obedience is the placing of the entire dynamism of the person at the service of the common good. This placing of ourselves in the service of the common good requires that our ears be open to hear the appeals that come to us and that we make ourselves available to assume the consequences of our dependence on the different communities that have allowed us to exist or that allow us to subsist.

Whether this dependence be original (family, country) or the result of a choice (marriage, religious profession), man remains a debtor. He must give a voluntary response to the expectations of the groups of which he is a member, even if to do so means that he is obliged to renounce some personal dream or privilege.

Thus we have the ideal of interhuman relations. This ideal is based on the very nature of man. The example is given by Christ, the author of this nature. By giving it its sacred value, he ratifies the service of the common good in which the interdependence of men expresses the common destiny of all the children of God.

B. Awareness of what is implied by the attitude of obedience in concrete human situations and in collective life. Is the service of the common good admitted and understood? Even in the family, that basic community with its close ties, we sometimes see mutual relationships established on the basis of particular interests and of opposite personalities rather than in function of the fulfillment that each one would obtain from the search by all for the common good.

This is even truer on the level of larger communities, professional and economic, ethnic and political. We see mutual relationships established through an equilibrium of the forces of dissuasion much more than by the reciprocal aid to which beings who have a common destiny should orient themselves.

Thus, on all imaginable levels of community life, the principles

of each one for himself and of free enterprise are in fact substituted
for the principle of solidarity. Men are not obedient.

Did Christ's disciples testify to this? We must certainly recognize
the value and often the heroism of individual witness. We find in
Christians more than elsewhere a true flowering of generosity in the
service of the common good. But do we find in Christians more than
in other men the feeling for positive solidarity that the common good
requires?

It suffices to press a button or to turn a tap to have light, running
water, heat and power instantly. These conveniences, and many
others like gasoline, fresh fruit and vegetables the year round, are
made possible for modern man thanks to the existence of new types
of communities based not only on production and consumption but
also on the creation and upkeep of a network of distribution. The
consumer belongs to these communities. Without them it would be
difficult for him to live. As a Christian, does he wish to be able to assume the consequences of his dependence on these different communities?

Here we encounter a fact. Among Christians, even those who are
most generous and who give freely of themselves to works of assistance and mercy, very few have realized what their dependence on
the different communities issued from technology represents for
them. They regard this dependence simply as a factual relationship, one of rights and duties, of use and of payment. They try to
obtain from it the maximum amount of benefits at the minimum
cost. Meanwhile they assure themselves that "in all this there is
no sin." But they have little notion that this dependence can bring
with it other duties. How many are preoccupied by the problems
that are presented on the level of human life by the technical processes that make available so many conveniences for them?

Behind a lamp that is lit there is the day and night service of
technicians and maintenance men, linemen and supervisors of big
power dams. The carrying out of modern technological tasks makes
each individual the beneficiary of the work, the vigilance, and the
application of a multitude of other individuals. It is a prodigious
enlightenment of the condition of obedience, outside of which the people could not live.

Never before has it been so necessary for man to keep his ears open, ready to hear the calls that come to him from his fellowmen. To give himself to this situation is for man to act according to the truth of his human condition. For the Christian, it is the first testimony to render to Christ (cf. 2 Cor. 4, 2), a testimony to be given before works of relief, of assistance, and of mercy. This fidelity to act according to the reality of our human condition has taken on a divine value since Christ lived it here below with an ear open to the calls that came to him from men.

C. Humanity obtains its common good from the practice of this ideal of obedience and it expects Christians to testify to it. The testimony borne by Christ in the course of his life on earth has accomplished a real revolution in the history of men.

Two thousand years after Christ, the forefront continues to be occupied by the ambitious and the swindler, and we see the lavish publicity of stars of all categories at the service of world wide audiences. There are also the others who lead lives of impersonation in front of their local audiences. They imagine that they are leading the world and they lull themselves with the satisfaction of "writing history."

In reality, history is written by the millions of lives that go on day after day in the service of the common good, often in the silence of a giving of self that is all the less noticeable as it is the more real and total. There is an immense multitude of the simple-hearted at the service of the common good in household activities and in the tasks of manual labor. Many also are responsible and hold essential posts in economic or administrative life. They, too, serve the common good. Nor must we forget the intellectuals at the service of the common good in the anonymity of research projects that publicly or privately seek to improve life. All of them in the measure that they are animated by the will to serve the common good in their respective places are living in true obedience.

Some do not know Christ. They are nonetheless in this service of the common good the beneficiaries of the reversal operated by Christ in the human conscience. As for those who have the happiness of knowing Christ they are in a better position to understand the value of their tasks, and they must oblige themselves to assume them all the better (cf. Rom. 13, 5).

This is to show the importance of the part that Christians must play in the true history written by men.

Technology has inaugurated among men an interdependence that becomes more and more cohesive. It can result in creating and imposing new forms of slavery. This can happen if each one sees in it only a source of individual convenience. It can also promote awareness of universal human solidarity. For this to happen, it will be necessary for each one of us to apply himself to see in the servitudes brought about by the application of technology the expression of the love that all men bear one another because each one of them is dear to the other.

It is from Christ that men can learn to regard each other in this way. For this to occur, Christians testifying for Christ must never dissociate themselves from those with whom they follow a common destiny in some life relationship. Following Christ they must know how to take upon themselves with love the burden, a fruit of sin, which often accompanies the establishment of a true human relationship. This is the task of Christians: to leaven the world.

This task must be assumed at a dual level, individually and collectively. It must be realized at the individual level in their personal relationships with those that are close to them: close to them by blood or culture, by work or play, through proximity or chance encounter. It must take place on the collective level, in the measure that they constitute in the world the visible Church in relation to all the needs in which, in some way, the life of the world is expressed.

Attentive to others, ears open to all appeals, Christians will then live in obedience. And this obedience will allow them to continue Christ's work here below. By restoring interhuman relations in the perspective of the common good they will have made this world what it is in reality, a preparation for the Kingdom of God. And perhaps they will even taste the joy of discerning in this world through a few insights, the prefiguration and the real establishment of the Kingdom, where all is peace.

Conclusions: Obedience restores the universe.　　The first nine verses of the eleventh chapter of Genesis tell the story of the tower of Babel.

In them, we see God represented in the most primitive traits formulating his plan as he views the enterprises of men: "Come, let us go down, and there confuse their language, that they may not understand another's speech."

This confusion of tongues (attributed to God as it would be in a primitive mentality) teaches a profound lesson. Men wishing to make a name for themselves, that is, wishing to become the center of their own activities made themselves incapable of understanding one another.

The opposite of the men of Babel, Christ, submits himself to men his brothers. He who is the Word of God enters into the web of interhuman relations. He accepts dependence on community realities in which all human life finds its support; he makes himself obedient.

Now, this obedience brings him a name "that is above all names" (Phil. 2, 9). After his resurrection, Christ communicated to men the Spirit that made it possible for them to understand each other even when they did not speak the same language.

The tower of Babel and the cross are two opposing images that impose a choice. Their opposition tells man that there is no restoration of the world into unity without obedience; that is, it can only come about through men showing fidelity to one another, and this even when it is difficult to live with one another, and when the choice to continue their unity in the community of their lives and destinies must come before themselves.

Francis of Assisi understood this because he had lived it painfully through the conflicts that developed in the interior of his order. "He who prefers persecution to separation from his brothers," he writes, "is he who truly remains in perfect obedience because he sacrifices his life for his brothers." This thought is in accord with the testimony given by Christ: Obedience is crucifying.

But beyond all torture and all death on the cross, obedience restores unity and life. In the measure that each man will have been attentive to his fellowmen just as one is attentive to a real word of God, a new being will be elaborated in the life of men, a reality more sacred than the earthly life of the Son of God (cf. 2 Cor. 5, 16-17). This reality is the total Christ, the true and ultimate common good of men, the fruit of true obedience inspired by love.

SECOND REFLECTION ON THE THEME
He Was Obedient to His Fellowmen

A. POINTS FOR MEDITATION

1. The filial relationship to the Father necessarily involves the child in the responsibilities of the business of the Father (cf. Lk. 2, 49). The business of the Father is above all the common good of men, his children. Every effort toward relationship with God that dissociates itself from the common good of men must be questionable to anyone who claims friendship with Christ.

2. This common good of men is not to be left to the imagination or to the kind heart of each one of us. It must be sought through the appeals expressed by present and future human realities.

3. This common good of men requires at the same time renouncement of self and the will to be as effective as possible. Thence comes the extreme gravity of two of its basic conditions: competence and professional conscience. This common good of men has been revealed to us as sacred by the choice Christ made of it in preference to his own life.

4. The common good of men is not good done to men; neither is it simply common interests. It is the Kingdom of God, that is, the institution among men of truly human relationships giving to each man the possibility of being fully a man as befits a child of God.

B. PARTICULAR THEMES

Choice of a career. Every man owes it to himself to seek a career in which his aptitudes and qualities will allow him to make the best contribution to the common good of men. This could mean giving up certain privileges and dreams of class consciousness.

Religious communities. Christians who are generous of heart can show as a collectivity reactions that are far from generous. Such and such a community is interested in the common good only to the degree that its own interests are involved. The natural communities to which its members belong seem to be nothing more than a

set of relationships with which it is important to deal wisely enough
to be able to reap from them maximum advantages at minimum cost
(family, locality, service groups, social security, etc.).

A general remark. The introduction into religious communities
of modern, time-saving devices for housework is accomplished with
a total indifference for the problems of social and economic life. We
have here a human group that benefits from all the advantages of
socialization while reserving for itself the independence of the arti-
san-rural rhythms of life proper to the past. Perhaps it will be said
that they have no other obligations because they pay their bills. This
is like the case of the man who performs his Easter duties and who
in his annual confession finds nothing of which to accuse himself
(aside from missing Mass and neglecting his prayers) because, as
he so aptly expresses it himself, "he has nothing to do with others."

C. Texts for Reading and Prayer

a. Biblical Texts

Lk. 6, 17 to end of chapter. See the link between the beatitudes and
the common good of men. Compare with Jn. 13, 17.

Jn. 13, 1-20. Jesus the servant of all. Compare with 2 Cor. 5, 16—6, 2;
1 Tim. 2, 1-8; Heb. 2, 10ff.

1 Cor. 8, 7—9, 26. Paul is aware of his rights but prefers not to use
them in favor of the common good. (Cf. 1 Cor. 9, 19-23 and Rom. 14.)

Eph. 4, 17—5, 21. New life established in Christ.

Lk. 10, 30-36. The two denarii. The love of God and the love of neighbor give to wounded man his full recovery in the inn that is the
Church.

b. Books

Thomas of Celano. *Vita Prima.* Part I, chaps. 16-21.
St. Francis. *Letter 3.*

c. Prayers

Ps. 22. Christ prayed with these words.
Ps. 33. Conditions of happiness.
Ps. 112. Praise for the just who is open to the calls of others.
Ps. 118. Christ, victorious over death, the salvation of all.

Final Theme

Heb. 3, 6. His dwelling is within us.

II

In Testimony to the God of Love

"I know Jesus poor and crucified, and that is
enough for me"

Francis of Assisi

"HE LEARNED OBEDIENCE THROUGH WHAT HE SUFFERED . . ." (Heb. 5, 8).

A. In his passion, Christ overcame all his repulsions, even the most legitimate, so as not to separate himself from the brothers his Father had given him.

"O Lord, thou hast deceived me and I was deceived; thou art stronger than I, and thou hast prevailed" (Jer. 20, 7).

The butt of persecutions that his part as a prophet has earned for him from other men causes Jeremiah to complain bitterly. He regrets that he has allowed God to do as he would with him, and regards himself as a dupe. He is angry with himself for having obeyed the Lord.

"I have become a laughing stock all day, every one mocks me . . . For the word of the Lord has become for me a reproach and derision all day long" (Jer. 20, 7-8). So the prophet has considered giving up altogether. (It is of no profit in any case.) ". . . I say 'I will not mention him, or speak any more in his name.' "

But he has hardly considered this solution when he recognizes in advance that it is an impossible one. He knows very well that he cannot keep inside himself the message he has been entrusted to proclaim. "There is in my heart as it were a burning fire shut up in my bones, and I am weary with holding it in, and I cannot" (Jer. 20, 9).

The Church likes to view in Jeremiah one of the most perfect prefigurations of the Lord, Jesus Christ. Like Jeremiah, Jesus has

74

known contradiction and mockery. Like Jeremiah, he has deeply felt weariness in the face of incomprehension (cf. Mt. 17, 16; Lk. 22, 42), and anguish grips him (cf. Lk. 12, 50; Jn. 12, 27). But far more than Jeremiah, Jesus carried within himself a "devouring fire," the incoercible need to spread the message he had the mission to reveal (cf. Lk. 12, 49).

Through the person of Jeremiah, we are introduced here to one of the most mysterious elements of the inner life of Christ Jesus, the combat whose theater was his heart and whose stake was the Yes that human nature in him had to give to the undertakings of God. To the culminating episode of this combat as it was lived out in the garden of Gethsemane, we have given the name of "agony." There, in the silence of the night and in the loneliness of his heart, Christ found himself in a certain way to be at grips with his own human weakness, like other men, made of flesh as they are, the butt of the fear and the panic of his own feelings before the images that in proximity of his hour had flooded his mind. He wept from anguish and cried out in fear (cf. Heb. 5, 7). His innermost self in the convulsions caused by the paroxysm of his struggle expressed its *fiat* only at the cost of a sweat of blood.

The outward and spectacular elements of the agony of Gethsemane can enlighten us on the meaning to be given to the reactions of our own human nature faced with the difficulties and trials of existence. If Christ had to overcome such paroxysms of resistance aroused in his inner self by the approach of the end, it was because everything in his being loathed the humiliations, the suffering, and above all, death. The life of the Lord (let us recall his tears before the tomb of Lazarus in Jn. 11, 35) confirms the justness of the recoil by which our nature reacts to everything that degrades it, alters it, or threatens it with destruction.

Now in this just recoil of his threatened human being, Christ had on his side all the reasons to defend himself that were given to him by his perfect innocence. The *fiat* he was required to pronounce was not a Yes given to a strictly personal situation. It was the Yes he had to give to a situation in which he was implicated only by solidarity with our human condition of sin.

Nonetheless, despite the just resistances that were thus stirring within his human nature, Christ did not allow himself to be stopped.

More than humiliation, suffering, and death, the very idea of not being faithful to the Father was insufferable to him: "There is in my heart as it were a burning fire . . . and I am weary with holding it in and I cannot" (Jer. 20, 9). On the level of reason and will, his human nature chose the passion which everything else in him rejected. To act otherwise would have been for this nature to cease to be itself. "My life is to do the will of him who sent me" (Jn. 12, 27, 28; 14, 31; 4, 34; 5, 30; 6, 38; 8, 29). To accomplish his Father's will was not to lose any of those his Father had given to him. (Cf. Jn. 6, 37-39.). So as to lose no one and to omit no one, Jesus had to consent in advance to all the situations that would come to him from the sole fact of his belonging to a world of men married by sin (cf. Heb. 2, 2).

B. By refusing no part of the human context that crushes him, Jesus gives testimony to God the Father, who is a God of Love. Chapters 50, 52 from verse 13 on, and 53 of the prophet Isaiah outline the portrait of the Servant. They already foretell the unbelievable fate that will be encountered by him who will come among men as witness to the love of a Father—God.

"Who has believed what we have heard? And to whom has the arm of the Lord been revealed?"

The prophetic texts do not spell out the price fixed in advance for men's ransom. They express as lived or foretold by such and such a prophet that to which, in advance, was destined he who would render testimony to the truth among men; that is, he who would live in conformity to the truth that God is love. For this witness to a God of love living in the midst of a world heavy with the weight of sin, destiny was predictable. Fidelity to love would doom him to incomprehension and hostility, to suffering and to death.

"Let us oppress the needy just man," are the words attributed to the impious by the Book of Wisdom (2, 10-22). The Church, during Passiontide, likes to apply these words to the situation in which Christ found himself in the midst of the horde of his adversaries. "He boasts that God is his Father . . . Let us test him with insult and torture . . . Let us condemn him to a shameful death." It sufficed for Christ to be the Holy One of God, the living manifestation of the Father who is Love to be doomed to this hostility.

At the same time as he is doomed to hostility, he is also compelled by his very holiness not to be able to reply to it otherwise than by fidelity to himself and to his Father, in silence. "He was oppressed and he was afflicted, yet opened not his mouth" (Is. 53, 7).

Charged with revealing the love of God, Christ entered into this world pledged in advance to the downfall of the passion.

One can say that these crushing humiliations were already inscribed in the first cell of the body of Christ formed by the Holy Spirit in the womb of the virgin. The fatal outcome of the Passion was in germ in the very first moments of the incarnation.

Christ did not reject this outcome: "I was not rebellious, I turned not backward. I gave my back to the smiters and my cheeks to those who pulled out my beard; I hid not my face from shame and spitting" (Is. 50, 5, 6).

In other words, he never allowed the will to love of which he had come to testify to be submerged even by the worst situations that could be made possible for him through the human context of his existence.

This, indeed, was the testimony that Christ had to give. To do so according to the truth of his human condition he had to keep himself available to the destiny that the logic of human situations prepared for him. In a hard and difficult world (the political and religious world of Judea occupied by the Romans and divided into rival factions), he who was the Son "had to be made like his brethren in every respect" (Heb. 2, 17) without having recourse to the "legion of angels" so as to bend the course of events to his own advantage (cf. Mt. 26, 53).

In his passion above all, he did not himself regulate the detail of the actions as one regulates the course of a scenario that has been planned in advance. He entered into it, accepting the drama as it was elaborated through the hatreds of its participants and of the cowardice or ambitions of others. "But I," said Jeremiah, "was like a gentle lamb led to the slaughter. I did not know it was against me they devised schemes."

The Word of God, Christ, was not ignorant of the plots woven by his enemies. The lamb of God, he consented to their normal human outcome. He did nothing to extricate himself from the situation with the least possible harm to himself, nor did he even try to shed a more favorable light on the fatal outcome to which the logic of events was leading him. He consented to a death in which he was only the victim of one of those irrational mob movements of which history records examples on each one of its pages. Although he was the Son, he learned through suffering how hard it is for man to live in a state of subjection that submits him to absurd situations, suffering, and death.

To submit oneself to such a destiny was impossible without an inward struggle.

In this struggle, Christ, the true Israel, was striving with God with all the rights of his innocence and all the holiness of his human nature assumed by the Word. Nonetheless, he allowed himself to be overcome . . . "who though he was in the form of God did not count equality with God a thing to be grasped, but emptied himself" (Phil. 2, 6).

Conclusions: To welcome others just as they are is a testimonial to our Faith in a God who is a Father.

To show himself until the end to be "the Son of God who is a Father" Christ loved his fellow-men, his own, "to the end" (Jn. 13, 1).

Placing himself within the love with which he loves his Father, he responded unto the end to the cries that came to him from the human world. For him these appeals were stronger than the fear of suffering, humiliation, and death.

But we know the cost of that struggle as Jesus thus submitted his life to the common good of men (cf. Heb. 5, 7). This cruel agony is an encouragement to us when we find it hard to surmount our own difficulties, weariness, temptations, and refusals. The difficulty we have in admitting what others are, and perhaps what others do to us, is easily a cause for discouragement. "I'll never arrive at it," is often heard. And one drags along, exhausting oneself in the struggle with inner resistances, wondering if he will ever manage to overcome them.

At these moments when one would like to feel oneself more generous and more courageous, it is the time to place ourselves in the context of the agony of the Lord. Because the difficulties that we have to admit certain situations is a part of this holy agony, we must live the difficulties we have as a participation in the struggle by which the Lord overcame even the most legitimate resistances within himself.

He who in all humility wills himself to be within the agony endured by Jesus will end one day by becoming capable of pronouncing his own *fiat*. It will be given to him to see clearly enough that others are his true brethren so that he will be able to love them with Christ and with the love with which the Father loves them. And the price that he pays for this love will not be a subject of regret, but will be for him the much prized proof that victory did not come from himself but was given to him from the Lord.

"I speak to thee . . . on the subject of thy soul," writes Francis of Assisi to one of his brothers who desired to be relieved of the charge of a community, "that those things which impede thee in loving the Lord God and whosoever may be a hindrance to thee, whether brothers or others, even though they were to strike thee— all these things thou shouldst reckon as a favor. And so thou shouldst desire and not otherwise. And let this be to thee for true obedience from the Lord God and from me, for this I know surely to be true obedience."

That which it costs us to obey is then no longer the sign of our condition of sin but the testimony given by our wills to remain with Christ within the love of the Father who loves us.

FIRST REFLECTION ON THE THEME
In Testimony to the God of Love

A. Points for Meditation

1. The death of Christ on the cross is one of those absurd events that a simple material incident (illness of the judge, a storm dispersing the crowd, etc.) would have averted.

2. To situate oneself within the love with which God loves us is to reject nothing of the interplay of events that is given us to live. There is no fatality and no chance.

3. To situate oneself in the love with which God loves us makes

it, above all, impossible to dissociate ourselves from any human being.

4. We can have a thousand good reasons not to have anything to do with a certain person or group. Nonetheless, we must never consider as broken the bonds that link us to these persons and even less must we consider these persons as non-existent.

5. Christians must forgive everything. It can happen that we are unable to suppress the bitterness or the inner revolt aroused in us by the very memory of such a person or such an event. This does not mean that we have not forgiven. A full pardon is compatible in us with the persistence of a whole universe of inward suffering. It is a participation in the agony of Jesus.

6. He whose charitable actions are inspired by human considerations risks despising men all the more as life reveals the better to him their smallness and miseries. He who is inspired by the example of Christ will be made capable of loving men even more if their smallness and their miseries become for him the occasion of greater suffering.

7. In a Christian heart, love for humanity is not illusion about humanity but an exact knowledge of the price of humanity.

8. It is not evangelical to make our services and our generosity spectacular (all the same, they ought to be known). We do not then proclaim the great Good News of a God of love but only the good news of our own personal actions.

"SOURCE OF ETERNAL SALVATION
TO ALL WHO OBEY HIM. . . ." (Heb. 5, 9)

A. Relations with others are the testimony to be given of our faith in a God of love the God who is Father of Jesus Christ. The testimony given by Christ in his agony enlightens the meaning of our existence here below. This existence is really an agony, a combat.

In this combat, man must accept himself just as events and the passage of time have allowed him to come into being. But no one comes into being alone. Man must therefore also accept himself in the web of relations and in the social context that is made for him by other men just as they are. By this attitude man testifies that he believes in a God who is a Father, a God of love and God of Jesus Christ.

In the logic of this faith, we must welcome all that comes to us from others and by others—confrontations with weakness and also with malice, servitudes and clashes that accompany the opposition of personalities, misunderstandings and incompatibilities that wound and sometimes divide beings who should be one. In these situations one must testify to belief in a God who is a Father.

On the other hand this testimony will have value only if it is given in the truth. Its value will be nothing if it is given under conditions that are falsified, in a way that seems to eliminate problems. The game of life must be played in all honesty without falsity and without sidestepping uncomfortable realities.

But falsity is often convenient, and it is sometimes practical to evade the issues. We organize things so that we are not inconvenienced. We make sure not to know things when we should. We advance so-called religious or supernatural arguments that allow us to avoid embarrassing situations in the name of superior obligations (cf. Mk. 7, 2). We ask for miracles to change situations (cf. Mt. 26, 53) and when this fails, we arrange for men to do the job.

We have touched here the depths of the imperatives of the Good News. The Good News, in which *we must believe,* of a God who is a Father (the God of Jesus Christ) requires of us that nothing that is in another or by another should be ignored, cursed, or destroyed. To all this the Father has given and will continue to give being. It is therefore with all this that we must live as sons of the same Father, without reproaching the Father for having given us certain of our brothers (cf. Mt. 13, 30).

Now, man often finds himself imprisoned in the complex and sometimes overwhelming texture of events for which others are responsible, as the fruits of a past in which he has had no part and are already heavy with the demands of a future in which he will have no part. He is subjected to situations that are the result of human intrigue and he is submitted to manifestations of the will of God expressing itself by and through the sins of others.

We understand then the cost of bearing testimony in our relations with others to our own faith in the God of love, God the Father announced by his Son, Jesus Christ, and we also understand the meaning of the testimony given by Christ in his passion. In consenting to the relations prepared for him by his human context, Christ was fully aware that his consent made him the witness of the true God of love who is a Father (cf. 1 Tim. 6). In his defeat and in his death it is God his Father whom he definitively obeys.

B. In the difficult response we must make, we have the example left by Christ.

There are situations when we need all the weight of this testimony of the Lord so as not to let ourselves be led into negation, doubt, or despair.

To welcome into our family a small malformed being, to accept into the context of our immediate and habitual relationships an individual whose sole encounter turns our blood to ice because he evokes too many things for us, to go to see such and such a person, or to maintain contacts with another as is required of us by claims from which we cannot escape—these are sometimes perspectives in life which of themselves are unbearable to contemplate. The day when these perspectives—sometimes at an hour and in a manner that was least expected—open up before us, our imaginations and feelings are quick to ask for less arduous ways, and reason comes to the rescue to justify these demands logically and to give its own guarantee to all other choices.

The Christian in such hours can understand through living it in his flesh what Christ came to bring him in submitting to the folly of the cross.

We must often recall to ourselves how Jesus accepted himself beneath the weight of existence. We must view him surmounting all the just revolts to which his imagination and sensitivity could have been surrendered. To follow him in this choice that leads him to prefer not his own will, however holy, but the will of his Father as expressed in the occurrence, is a source of truth about ourselves. What a light is projected on our most complex situations! What powerful reasons are thus given to us to make us wish to be faithful ourselves to that context of human relations in which it has been given to us to live. So must we be faithful to every event that manifests itself in the traits of a brother and keep ourselves available to live whatever we must live, even if, in back, this will be overwhelming suffering.

Jesus in his passion makes possible for us to accept what is most difficult. To the condition of slavery in which man struggles is substituted for all those who follow him a condition of freedom. The man who espouses the *fiat* of the Lord becomes capable of accepting through love, and therefore freely, even that which he could very legitimately refuse.

As he advances into life, each man discovers, day after day, that new demands are made of him, and that reasons for avoiding them are not lacking. But the disciple of Christ, instead avoiding the servitudes through which his faith in a God of love is expressed wills himself to be more completely submissive to them from day to day. To act otherwise is impossible for him; he would cease to be himself: "There is in my heart as it were a burning fire . . ." The fidelity he has manifested by testifying to his faith in a God who is a Father has given him back to himself by effectuating the unity of his being in Christ. This unity allows him to taste, even while he suffers, a true happiness. He knows himself to be saved already along with all those who inspire themselves with the example of Christ (cf. Heb. 5, 9).

C. Evangelical value of the testi-   *"De patre creditur, interposita*
mony given to God by accept-   *matris auctoritate."* This mysteri-
ance of others.   ous phrase written by St. Augus-
tine is replete with significance.
The Father, that is, God, no one has ever seen (cf. Jn. 1, 18).
Nevertheless, all men form for themselves some idea of God even if
this idea is the equivalent of "nothingness."

Now the idea that they have of the Father men form from the
idea they receive from their Mother, the Church, and Christ is the
head of the Church. Since Christ, the mother is every baptized member of the Church. All of the baptized, each one as an individual,
and all of the baptized to the degree that they form a collectivity,
must live in such a way as to be able to say what Christ was able to
say: "He who sees me sees the Father" (Jn. 14, 9).

For the Christian, the question is a serious one. What relationship
does the Church (the Mother) have with other men through my
person? From my relations with them, with others (first of all with
those near to me) are they inclined to form an idea about God that
corresponds to reality, an idea of a God who is love, and who is a
Father?

Now for the man, the reply to this question is decisive. The child
submits himself positively to the demands of education only to the
degree that he is profoundly conscious of being loved by those who
educate him. Man (as individual and as society) can only enter positively into his own existence to the degree that he is deeply aware
that in all the servitudes which accompany life he is loved by the
being from whom all things come.

The deep awareness of being loved does not come to a child
because he has been loaded with gifts or is the object of sweet
words. So it is for man in relation to God. Faced with miracles, gaz-
ing at the formula, "God is Love" written in letters of fire in the
darkness of the heavens, man in his days of defeat could still deny
God and even curse him. Only the crucified Son allows man to know
that he is loved (cf. Rom. 5, 8; 8, 32 ff.). Faced with Christ on the
cross, man can form the most exact idea about God: God is a Father.
He is love.

But it is necessary for men that the testimony of Christ should be prolonged by the testimony of the baptized and as much by individual testimony as by the worldwide testimony given by the Church in its relations with the world. The proclamation of the Good News depends on this

CONCLUSIONS

To believe that God is love does not open the way to some form of easy religious sentimentality.

To believe that God is love engages man in the total integration of his own person with the destiny of his fellowmen for the salvation of all even if this demands some personal defeat for him (cf. 1 Jn. 3, 16).

Man on his own would be incapable of such an engagement, but in his agony Christ gave value to all our struggles. He sanctified even those states of utter depression to which we see ourselves reduced in the effort to overcome resistances within ourselves. Beyond these states of depression, his grace makes us capable of welcoming everything that can be asked of us by interhuman relationships. We find in Christ the road to our own personal unity and the road to our unity with all other men, welcomed and loved as brothers and as sons of the same Father (cf. 2 Cor. 5, 14-15).

In the most trying moment of the life of his Order, Francis of Assisi found himself the butt not only of the weakness but even of the opposition of a good number of those in whom he had placed his trust, the ministers. Faced with the difficulties that this opposition aroused, he thought of allowing the majority of the brothers to follow their own way while for his part he walked the rough road with his more generous companions of the first hour. He always rejected this idea as a temptation. One day when these trials became overwhelming one of the brothers proposed to cheer him up by reading to him from one of the prophets. Francis then gave this admirable reply: "I know Jesus poor and crucified, and that is enough for me."

"O Lord, thou knowest," writes Jeremiah, "that for thy sake I bear reproach. Thy words were found and I ate them and thy words became to me a joy and the delight of my heart. For I am called by thy name, O Lord God of Hosts" (Jer. 15, 15-16).

To bear his name is, with the grace of Jesus and by following him, to live in such a way that those around us can believe that God is love.

SECOND REFLECTION ON THE THEME
In Testimony to the God of Love

A. POINTS FOR MEDITATION

1. The death of Christ is written into the texture of human events on the same level as the news items reported in the daily papers.

In the event wherein Christ redeems us, the essential element is his considered and voluntary consent to the human context in which as Son of man he finds himself implicated.

2. The filial relationship of the Christian to God is necessarily inscribed in a context of sin that dooms the Christian to be like Christ a sign of contradiction in the midst of men.

To be a sign of contradiction does not mean to judge and condemn sin and sinners. It means to live in such a way that to sin, the practical negation of love, should be opposed. Its contradiction, holiness, is the only valid and practical affirmation of love.

3. To believe that God is love is to have faith. It does not mean to count firmly on God to perform the miracles necessary to make everything work out best for our own immediate interests. Neither does it not mean to count on a special attention from the protective services of the Almighty as they are expressed in some good-natured ruler.

4. All the acts that I perform must express a filial relationship to God. So-called religious acts may express only a mercenary relationship. "Lord, you have received your dues, now don't forget to give me mine." On the contrary, this filial relationship is abandonment of self to God. It involves acceptation by faith of death with Christ. Acceptance of this death testifies to our belief in a God of love who can even resurrect the dead (cf. Heb. 11, 19).

5. A true fidelity to the condition of obedience, which is that of the human family because of sin, necessarily implies perspectives of

renunciation for the individual. Dialogue can inside of existing communities diminish tensions and attenuate causes of conflict; it will never restore the state of original justice. A human community, even a religious community will always be a community of sinners. The common good can only prevail in them at the cost of self-sacrifice by which their members testify to their FAITH in a God of love.

B. TEXTS FOR READING AND PRAYER

a. Biblical Texts

Ezek. 37, 15-28. Foreshadow of the Cross that restores unity that was broken.

Is. 63, 1-7. It is in his own blood that Christ is "in crimsoned garments."

Mt. 21, 33-42. It can cost dearly to be a son.

Jn. 3, 16-18. Mission of Jesus. Jn. 18, 28-38. Accomplished by his death.

Rom. 5, 1-12 and 8, 28-39. Certitude that God loves us in Christ.

1 Jn. 4, 7-10. To love is the only true wisdom. 1 Cor. 1, 17-2, 6. Christ is the witness to this wisdom of God.

Lk. 10, 30-36. Find in the gestures of the Samaritan the portrait that Jesus has painted for us of himself.

b. Books

Thomas of Celano, *Vita Prima*, Part II, chaps. 1-6.

St. Francis, *Rule*, 1, chaps. 9-11; *Admonitions*.

c. Prayers

Pss. 38; 55; 56; 57; 59. A call to God in the midst of contradictions.

Pss. 69; 88; 102. Christ lived these situations.

Pss. 13; 142. A prayer of a witness of the God of love.

Final Theme

Rom. 5, 8.

III

Thus Becoming Perfect

> If a mother nourishes and loves her carnal son,
> how much more earnestly ought one to love and
> nourish his spiritual brother.
>
> Francis of Assisi, *Rule,* 6

"AS CHRIST DOES (FOR) THE CHURCH" (Eph. 5, 29).

A. The image of Eve foretells the death of Christ from which we receive life.

The story of the creation of woman in the second chapter of Genesis is one in which the majority of the faithful do not suspect the symbolic riches.

"Then the Lord God said: 'It is not good that the man should be alone. I will make him a helper fit for him.' So the Lord God caused a deep sleep to fall upon the man and while he slept took one of his ribs and closed up its place with flesh. And the rib which the Lord God had taken from the man he made into a woman and brought her to the man. Then the man said: 'This at last is bone of my bone and flesh of my flesh; she shall be called woman because she was taken out of man.' Therefore a man leaves his father and his mother and cleaves to his wife and they become one flesh" (Gen. 2, 18.21.24).

This text has been widely commented upon by the Fathers of the Church. St. John Chrysostom in his "Homily to the Neophytes" likes to compare it with the 19th chapter of John the Evangelist. From the open side of the body of Christ, the true Adam, sleeping on the cross with the sleep of death, God has caused by the lance of the soldier a source of water and blood to spring forth carrying with it divine life to humanity.

In his work entitled *The Mystical Vine,* St. Bonaventure has also

88

given a commentary on the creation of Eve that is striking in its brevity. Just as the rib taken from the side of Adam caused the clay molded in the form of a woman to be recognized by Adam as flesh of his flesh and bone of his bones, so the water and blood flowing from the side of Christ pierced by the lance and mixed with the human dust molded by time causes this humanity to be recognized by Christ as flesh of his flesh and bone of his bones. Humanity become the Church attaches itself to Christ, and he attaches himself to humanity become the Church. The two form but one flesh, one sole being: the whole Christ (cf. Eph. 5, 30.33).

From the picture developed from the story of the creation of Eve, a lesson is given us. Just as Eve a "helpmate like to himself" came to existence through the sleep of Adam, so humanity is born to divine life through the death of Jesus on the cross.

B. The image of the Temple foretells the gathering together of men in the resurrection of Christ. Side by side with the story of Eve's creation can be placed the vision of the source flowing from the Temple in the 47th chapter of the prophet Ezekiel.

While the sons of Israel wept in exile and of the Temple built by Solomon there no longer remained stone upon stone, the prophet in a vision sees the restored Temple erect before him. In the course of his visit to the Temple, Ezekiel discovers a source.

"Water was issuing from below the threshold towards the East . . . and the water was flowing down from below the south end of the threshold of the Temple, south of the altar . . . and the water was coming out on the south side" (Ezek. 47, 1.2). This water is described by the prophet as becoming a stream, a torrent, a river that finally widens out and loses itself in the sea. It teems and swarms with fish and on its banks life manifests itself in uninterrupted growth and harvests because the water for them flows from the sanctuary.

The Temple seen by Ezekiel in the place of the Temple of Solomon ruined by the enemies of Israel recalls the mysterious words of Jesus to his enemies who asked him for a sign "Destroy this temple and in three days I will raise it up," he spoke, notes St. John, of the temple of his body (Jn. 2, 18-22).

The vision of Ezekiel foretells Christ's death and resurrection. It

also foretells the flow of blood and water from his side. Christ in
the mystery of his death is the true temple of God destroyed by
men and rebuilt in three days. From this true temple of God there
flows the source that carries divine life to men through the sacraments.

The water flowing from the altar, announced by the prophet
Zechariah (cf. Zech. 13, 1) was promised to the Samaritan woman
(cf. Jn. 4, 14) and to the Jews (cf. Jn. 7, 37.39). St. John, the evangelist who tells us of these promises is also the witness who saw their
accomplishment. From the side opened by the lance he saw with
his own eyes the water and blood flow forth (cf. Jn. 19, 34-35).
The Church invites us to make these comparisons. During Easter-
tide in the celebration of the mystery of our entry into life through
the waters of baptism, she sings each Sunday: "I saw water flowing
out of the right side of the Temple . . ."

C. The admirable exchange whose   The story of the creation of
condition is our "destruction."   Eve and the vision of the source
Christ is "established" by our   flowing from the Temple cut
restoration.   across each other in the development of their imagery.

Thanks to the water, dust becomes dough that can be kneaded,
thanks to the ferment of life represented by the rib, the dough becomes a living creature.

It remains for us to consider more deeply through these images
the relations that unite us to Christ and through Christ to other men.

These images lead us to understand, first of all, that Christ in his
life and death accepted himself as conditioned by us. He lives and
"constructs" himself because of the multitude of the variable creatures that are men. Instinctively, every man wishes to "live his life,"
"to make himself." Christ consents to "make himself" only for
others.

He even accepts his own destruction in time (destroy this temple . . .) because it is necessary for the eternal construction of
redeemed humanity (I will rebuild it in three days . . .).

The rib that made of Eve a living being could be taken from
Adam only during his sleep. The source that carries life into the
desert could only flow from the open side at the price of death. It

was necessary for Christ to accept his own destruction for our restoration to become possible.

But this is only the first part of an admirable exchange. Christ who thus accepts his own destruction for us comes to the fulness of his being established only through us. He becomes perfect, finished, achieved, accomplished in his final totality only because the men born from his death to real life give themselves as living stones for the construction of the eternal temple willed by God (cf. 1 Chr. 2, 5). This eternal temple, center of the universe, the beginning and the end of all things, enters into the full development of itself only in its integration into our condition of degradation, associated with our sin even unto death (cf. Heb. 2, 10; 5, 7; 2 Cor. 1, 19.20).

We can understand here in its totality the undertaking that subjected Christ totally to the common good of men.

Christ wished himself to be subjected to the common good of men because as son of Mary, he inherited his humanity from the human race. But this submission of his being to the common good came also because Christ knew that his own achievement could only come from a total solidarity with the world of men.

The solidarity that binds Christ to the human race makes him see in the world of men the indispensable self-complement without which he would not feel that he achieved his purpose. He thinks of each man as each man thinks of his own body. "It is flesh of my flesh, bone of my bone."

Conclusions: Christ in the images of Eve and the Temple reveals to us the final meaning of our relations with others.

Our reflection on the attitude of Christ with his ears open finds its culmination here. We are led beyond a simple acceptance of the difficulties that often accompany our beginning relations with others. We see the burdens borne because of others and with them, the acquiescence that comes from social life, the confrontations with the weaknesses and even the malice of others. We also become aware of the encounters and situations that exert determining pressures on the course of our lives and realize these enable us to achieve selfhood. Through all of them a new being is elaborated. Christ prolongs in us who are his members the attitude of obedience to men that brought him to the realization of himself in the mystery of his death on the cross.

There are situations when the burden of social relationships become heavy for a man. The network that should normally carry him along comes to the point of enclosing him, paralyzing him, and sometimes of stifling him. When these situations are the result of his existence, man fears instinctively and above all else, a diminution of himself.

The Christian knows that these situations, if by misfortune they fall to him, do not risk self-diminution. While feeling them very painfully in his heart, he knows how to expect from them in Christ a more perfect self-realization. In effect, the destiny lived by Christ tells us that the full and perfect realization of the persons we are must be found in the integration of one's whole self with the situations and experiences of other men.

Far from seeing in the struggles in which we are engaged on account of others obstacles to our perfection, we see in them the crucible wherein our condition as sons of God is elaborated and perfected. A solidarity that is really lived fosters possible development of the baptized person.

The spiritual tradition of Christianity has seen the importance of this living fellowship since its earliest times (cf. Acts 42, 47). The mutual relationships implied by all community living have a primordial place in the conversion of the heart, in the metanoia in depth of the sinners we are. The essential elements in my conversion are the mutual relationships in the interior of a community life.

To say, "if you want to suffer, live in a community," is not only a misconception but evident proof that we have forgotten the ecclesial dimensions of conversion and salvation. A whining individualism turns suffering into a sort of self-glorification. There are more human (St. Paul would say "carnal") motivations than Christian (St. Paul would say "spiritual") inspiration in the principles vaunted by some who aspire to perfection.

It is necessary to restore its true value of living fellowship to community life. Ecclesial life has as its one and supreme end the life of charity. It must not be a simple context, a receptacle in which each being lives out his own existence. All the relationships that are formed in it have life-value; by all of these relationships, the Spirit causes us to be born to the new life of Christ and of God.

St. Francis of Assisi understood this admirably. A simple phrase from his *Testament* reveals to what depths this consciousness had penetrated: "When the Lord had *given* me brothers . . ." he writes. In his brothers, he had been able to see gifts of God.

Through the mutual relationships that are provided for man by the different communities to which he belongs, his real being, far from running risks or suffering diminution, is saved and achieved. There, in truth, in the mystery of the body of Christ in the process of completing itself, the baptized can submit himself to the Spirit and accede to his own real perfection.

FIRST REFLECTION ON THE THEME
Thus Becoming Perfect

A. POINTS FOR MEDITATION

1. Life comes out of death.

2. Christ, the Word of God made flesh, exists as a man only from elements borrowed from the cosmos. He lived his life and his death in the logic of this dependence. Each man exists as he is only from elements borrowed from the cosmos (elements borrowed from the material world and elements borrowed from the human world of ideas, theoretical and practical knowledge, relationships, etc.). Truth is to live our lives in the logic of this dependence.

3. The essential elements of the elaboration in us of the personal image of God are the relationships of the social world. The essential elements of the restoration in us of this resemblance with God are the relationship inside of different human communities on all planes.

4. It is good to value the absolute dignity of the person, but we must not make the person an absolute. The person is only relatively absolute, for he exists only as a junction of relationships.

5. The value of the person does not depend so much on the multiplicity as on the quality of the relationships in which it elaborates

itself. In the measure that educators (parents and teachers) know how to respect this requirement, they can hope to fulfill their task properly.

6. There is no conceivable human situation wherein we cannot become more ourselves by the grace of Christ. For the grace of Christ makes us capable of finding materials for the elaboration of ourselves even in overwhelming situations.

7. The paradox and folly of Christ's passion—it inclines us to accept all burdens coming from others. It removes any desire ever to impose a burden on others.

"GROW UP IN EVERY WAY INTO HIM WHO IS THE HEAD"

A. Socialization and reevaluation of the community dimension of salvation. The meditation on texts in which the mystery of the Church is foreshadowed makes evident the essential part played by interhuman relations in the elaboration in us of the new being that is promised because it is the fruit of the Spirit.

Thus, the Christian who would imagine that he can grow in Christ while dissociating himself from those to whom he is bound in a common destiny does not recognize the reality in which salvation is carried out. Whether it be the community of destiny with those who are nearest to him (family, profession, country), or the community of destiny with those he never meets but who are encountered by his representatives on a level of higher proceedings, it is impossible for whoever wishes to live the mystery of Christ to dissociate himself from others. He can find his own achievement in Christ only through others.

The modern context of socialization has contributed to bring new recognition to this communal dimension of the mystery of Christ. The saying: "It is not good for man to be alone" (Gen. 2, 18), finds new emphasis in the realities of modern life.

By its complexity, modern life specializes human work ad infinitum. The diversification of the parts of a same activity or science makes it unthinkable for a man to concentrate in his head alone all knowledge or all power. "Man alone" has become an impossibility. The human social body has become a real organism; each human being must cooperate in the smooth workings of the whole by assuming a part that is often very precisely defined. Each community (professional, economic, political, or social, family group or religious society) must will itself to service the greater communities, who are themselves subject to the community that is humanity taken in its entirety.

The human race can only subsist through this voluntary convergence of the dynamisms of persons and groups formed by these persons. But to this convergence of forces rising below must correspond at the summit the conscience of a mission to be fulfilled. This is to assure each one of these various communities and through them to each of the persons of whom they are composed the most complete self-achievement.

An end has therefore come to the unconscious isolations in which individuals and collectivities, nations and continents formerly used to live. The socialization of life, an inevitable consequence of technical development, obliges men to take into consideration the community dimensions of their destinies.

Better than anyone else, the disciple of Christ can grasp the truth of this situation. By the demands that it, in fact, implies, the modern context of socialization can make interhuman relations more like the mystery of Christ. As they finally assume their universal dimensions, the realities of nature are revealed to correspond exactly to what God has revealed to us of the realities of grace (cf. Eph. 3, 18).

Besides this, the disciple of Christ is thus enabled to understand all that the example of Christ has given to him when he has recognized the demands of the present situation. This example is the perfect response to the expectations of men. From it the relations of dependence and the exercise of authority are restored to their truth.

B. Dependence and authority in service of "growth." Dependence and authority are correlative. The exercise of an authority consecrates in a certain manner the existence of relationships of dependence.

Authority, as the etymology of the word indicates, is the principle of growth. Through the exercise of authority to which a man submits himself or with which he is invested, he grows in all that by which he is a man.

The plant and the animal can attain the fullness of their development almost in complete isolation from their "likes." On the contrary, man, if he is to grow and fulfill himself to the utmost in that by which he is most deeply human, needs to be in relation with other human beings. These relations are necessarily made up of the correlative aspects of dependence and authority.

But authority is exercised according to God's plan only if it consecrates the relations of mutual dependence that are proper to the fulfillment of persons. The sign that authority is exercised according to God's will is not the law and order that may prevail in a given place. It is not even the well-being that is enjoyed there. Only the fullness of spiritual life that can be attained there by human beings is the testimonial that authority is carrying out its true function, which is to procure the growth of the body and of each member of this body.

In the mystery of the Church, "we are to grow up in every way into him who is the head, into Christ, from whom the whole body, joined and knit together by every joint with which it is supplied, when each part is working properly, makes bodily growth and up-builds itself in love" (Eph. 4, 15-16). Divine life increases in all of the body and in each member of the body because Christ has exercised his authority over us by submitting his person totally to the call of our common good.

Thus, he who wishes to assume authority in regard to other men must vow himself completely to the service of the true achievement of the group and of each member in it.

The true function of authority is not therefore to fill a vacancy (someone must do so) or to hold a rank (representation) but to promote the growth in each man of that which makes him most truly man.

There are many human groups in which authority tends to be exercised by a leader or leaders who are at the service of the growth of each and of all their members (research, education, cooperatives, etc.). Every human group (family, economical, professional, and political) in which natural realities are lived thus tends to a perfection of interhuman relations of which the mystery of the Church is the crowning point. These human groups because their authority is exercised within them according to God become true preparations for the mystery of the Church; the whole Christ is in formation in them through the exercise of an authority that coming from God, knows how to exercise itself, and respect the nature created by God.

On the other hand, it can happen that the formation of the whole Christ is rendered difficult or even impossible by the exercise of an authority in which nature is not respected. Let us not even mention the leader who takes advantage of his position to use others for his own ends.

But there is the case of those who think that because of their position they have the right, and even the duty, to place others at the service of their own ideas. There are also those who imagine that they are causing God to be adored by others because they have presented their own person to the homage of others.

Such a service of authority no longer has the fulfillment of others as its prime objective. The placing of others at the service of ends considered just or even religious does not change the situation. This intention cannot constitute an exercise of authority according to God. Its results go contrary to that which God intended when he instituted authority among men (cf. Rom. 13, 1 and Jn. 19, 2). The disregard of the respect due to nature ends by thwarting the fulfillment of charity and supernatural life.

It is thus that a human group, even though a religious community, in which the exercise of authority would limit itself to maintaining law and order and well-being would be only a superior type of zoological grouping. We would be dealing with a good business firm exceptionally well organized, or with a small store, but we would certainly not find in this human group the preparation or the living reality of the mystery of the Church.

C. Interdependence of men and the preparation of the Mystical Body in the mystery of the Church.   It is a commonplace to say that the depravations found in the exercise of authority are correlative to the depravations consented to in the acceptance of dependence. The Christian knows that these depravations in the very degree that they are prejudicial to some natural reality are at the same time prejudicial to the accomplishment of the mystery of the Church.

It is important for the collective situations brought about by the progress of technology for the men of today to be seen for what they are by the disciples of Christ. As a matter of fact, it is from this web of natural realities that the supernatural bonds, the works of the Spirit, are elaborated. "It is the spirit that gives life, the flesh is of no avail" (Jn. 6, 63).

This means that in the formation of one's person into a child of God the web of relations according to the Spirit is of more weight and import than the descendence according to the flesh. In this domain of the person, something is of value only in the measure that, as it should be, it is a carrier of the Spirit.

Now it depends on man that the flesh be a carrier of the Spirit, and by the term "flesh," man is obliged to include all the contexts of relationships in which he can live. There are not only relationships within the family, there are also the professional relationships, leisure activities, economics, politics, the neighborhood, and chance encounters. All these terrestrial realities which would be of no value to LIFE if they were limited to themselves become the very reality of LIFE. But this requires of us that we know, at one and the same time, how to accept them in their authenticity and to live them in submission to the Spirit.

To receive these earthly realities in their authenticity is to be faithful to nature; it is to integrate oneself to the rhythm of economic life, and to renounce the creation of "closed circuits" that allow one to escape the servitude of the whole while profiting from its efforts. It is to admit the existence of new types of human communities in which the characteristics are less those of implantation than of function in the service of a whole.

To live these earthly realities in submission to the Spirit is to approach them with the same attitude with which we would approach God, that is, by the exercise of theological virtues.

We must have the eyes of FAITH, for out of the fine dust of life's events is modeled the body of the eternal companion that God is preparing for Christ, the true Adam. We must keep HOPE in our hearts, for despite the present disillusions, humanity will be for Christ at the last day "a helpmate like to himself." We must live all things in CHARITY, for the dust of humanity becomes the living body in which Christ recognizes "the flesh of his flesh, the bone of his bones" because it is made from the water and blood that flowed from his wounded side. This means that the relations of interdependence of which human life is made become divine only if man assumes them in Christ and *with the love with which Christ loved.*

We already see here that a *bouleversement* of self can be for us the entry into a vision of all things bringing all things to Christ. A new meaning becomes apparent in each community situation that we are asked to live. For me, a Christian, others are Christ integrating me to his glory through my participation in his blessed passion (cf. Canon of the Mass; Phil. 3, 10-11). If they are not "Christ," they are (or they will be one day or another) "hell."

Whether it be a question of circumstances or of people, we spontaneously react by equating them with obstacles and nuisances. "If it were not for him . . ." "If it were not for that schedule," we say.

Now others or the situations created by others are in fact the components of the true fulfillment of my being. The grace that is given to me by Christ does not ignore any one of them. The grace that fulfills me and helps me grow in Christ embraces them also (cf. 1 Pet. 3, 8.17). There can be therefore no question of ignoring them, of eliminating them or even of neutralizing them. It is a matter of finding the way to integrate myself with them and if need be, of sacrificing myself for them.

This is the way opened by Christ who accepted his own destruction, who was the altar and the temple of God, so that he could integrate us to his eternal construction, we who are the stones. He who is life placed himself in our deaths to introduce us into his life, we who are the dead (cf. 1 Pet. 3, 8-19).

CONCLUSIONS

Christ is the perfect answer to all the expectations of men. Not only is he in his person the model human being, the perfect specimen of the individual but is also the reply to the questions in the heart of every man by the problems he finds in his relations with other men. To these problems and to the questions they bring with them, the only answer is to love with the love with which Christ loved.

"For if a mother nourishes and loves her carnal son how much more earnestly ought one to love and nourish his spiritual brother" (St. Francis of Assisi, *Rule,* 6).

The road indicated here by Francis of Assisi is indeed the path that God has opened up for men through his Son, a path foreshadowed in the images of Eve and the Temple and followed by Christ in the mystery of his death. I can dream of perfection, of holiness, of glory only through the integration of myself to all others, even at the cost of a sort of death to myself.

This undertaking of integration with others will express itself, first of all, by silence kept before others. Jesus kept the silence of Nazareth until he was thirty years old. His passion expresses above all an attitude of silence.

We must accept to remain silent for some time with others if we wish to hear them. True knowledge of others and their appeals is measured by the silence that one has the patience and courage to maintain in their presence. Only a true and loving silence can allow a human being to express himself with enough freedom for his own true appeals to be heard.

Whoever seeks to live his relations with others while remaining aware that they are Christ will be able to hear pronounced in his own life the word of God that others are.

SECOND REFLECTION ON THE THEME
Thus Becoming Perfect

A. POINTS FOR MEDITATION

1. The participation of a Christian in the mystery of the life of Christ cannot be situated outside of the human context in which he lives. To expect our progress in Christ from some event that is outside of the everyday life we lead is therefore a vain hope. Progress can be expected only from fidelity to the events of our habitual life. These "events" are to be found first of all in the fabric of relationships prepared for us by the reality of existence—in the family, professions, different communities.

2. He who wishes to live his life, to be a self-made man is exposed to being nothing more than a stunted creature at the end of his existence. He will never have become fully what he could have been (cf. Mk. 8, 35). This danger lies in wait more particularly for the Christian who is satisfied with his "religious practices." In fact, an attention to self that is not balanced by attentiveness to others fixates

a person at one stage of his development, and he doesn't go beyond himself.

3. To desire to be at peace is equivocal. One can, even in the solitude of the cloister be at peace with the peace that the world gives (individualism) while imagining oneself to be enjoying the peace promised by Christ (cf. Jn. 14, 27).

4. If my relationships are selected because of my simple concern to enjoy peace, then my situation is a dangerous one. "I lose my soul." If my relationships are chosen because of my will to establish charity in my interhuman relations I am in God's plan. "I gain my soul" (cf. Jn. 24, 25).

5. The "purity" of my relations with others conditions the degree of achievement that I shall attain in divine life. It is therefore important to give myself to the purifications that relations with others bring with them.

Let me reflect here very specially on the categories of persons with whom I keep up relations the most assiduously. What categories? Which persons? In those relationships that present no difficulties am I sure that I am not the prisoner of ready-made ideas, admitted prejudices, advantageous conveniences, and prejudices favorable to myself? Is this absence of difficulties a sign of communion or of rigid compartmentalizing, of truth loved in common or of lies consented to together?

B. Particular Themes

Clergy. On the subject of the team spirit. The need to form a team expresses the rediscovery of the community dimension of the ministry. On the diocesan level (ecclesial unity) the term forming a team has a synonym, "pastoral of the whole."

We must not regard this aspiration as a fad or simply as an ecclesiastical new look. It is a vital reaction against the suffocation due to individualism in the ministry. We must not see in team life something that is the concern of a minority who are following their temperaments. It is a matter of the constitution of the Church in its collegiality.

We must not see in the team a simple instrument of better efficacy in action. It is a condition of ecclesial authenticity. He who does not feel the need to be with others is not strong but weak in the Spirit of Christ, for he wants to satisfy himself by thinking that he can arrive on his own, whereas if he were strong in the Spirit of Christ, he would be delighted to be able to arrive only with others.

We must not see in the team something that we have to bear but a requirement for salvation. It is a question of self-achievement through placing self truly at the service of the Church.

Religious Life. It can happen that Christians aspire to community life or resign themselves to persevere in it because, all things considered, the advantages that are attached to it (a common purse, a roof and food for all, heat and seclusion and sick care assured for everyone) are well worth the few unpleasant features that must be accepted along with the rest. This attitude ignores the best that is given to the Christian by community life.

Relations with the world of unbelievers. A human being can in the course of his childhood and youth receive nothing from adults but lessons when he expects from them a loving silence attentive to the values he seeks to express. It will take much time after that for a dialogue without ill-humor to be established between this being who is now a man and those men who thought they were forming him. The modern world during the decades of its first expansion encountered from clerics warnings and condemnations far more often than loving attention to the values of progress and science that it was expressing within itself. Now it is for the clerics to know how to keep silent long enough for this negative past to be reabsorbed so that at last a true dialogue without resentment may be established between the modern world and the Church of Christ.

C. TEXTS FOR READING AND PRAYER

a. Biblical Texts

Gen. 39-50. The story of Joseph. Joseph, the image of Christ, makes himself known to his brothers only after having tested their affection for the youngest of them, Benjamin. Compare Gen. 64, 33 and Mt. 25, 40; Gen. 65, 5 and Jn. 14, 2.

Ruth (the entire book). The respect by a pagan for natural bonds is to give Israel the line from which one day Christ will come forth (cf. Ruth 1, 16; 4, 17).

Is. 11. Vision of the peace that Christ brings us.

Ezek. 67; Zech. 14, 8; Jn. 2, 13-23; 4, 10; 7, 37-40; 9, 31-36. Prefigurations of Christ, the Temple, and the Source of Life.

Lk. 10; 34: "He set him on his own beast."

Rom. 12, 3-21; 1 Cor. 12, 4-27; Eph. 4, 4-17. Affirmation and explanation of the solidarity of all men in the Body of Christ.

b. Books

St. Francis, *Rule,* 1, chaps. 6 and 7; *Admonitions.*

c. Prayers

The Psalms express a spiritual life that is little affected by the discovery of the other. Ps. 19 (humility); 25 (justice); 40 (the meaning of others); 67; 72; 87 (universal brotherhood of peoples). Compare also Rom. 8, 31ff.; Eph. 3, 14ff.; 1 Pet. 1, 3-9.

Final Theme

1 Pet. 2, 5.

PART TWO: CONCLUSIONS

The second word addressed by God to man is his fellowmen.

But this word of God is incomprehensible to man as long as he does not listen to it in the light of the Son of God made man.

Through CHRIST the Word of God made man, who became the perfect image of what every man should become, man can understand his destiny as a child of God (cf. Rom. 8, 29).

CHRIST conducted himself as a son (cf. Heb. 3, 6). By submitting himself to the COMMON GOOD of men he testified that God is a Father and that he attains his own achievement at the same time as he makes the fulfillment of every human being possible.

Through his insertion into the life of men at the price of his own life, CHRIST, the living Word of God, tells me that in each situation lived in relation with other men, testimony can be given to the truth that God is LOVE and that he is a Father.

This testimony is borne by the Christian when he remains attentive to the appeals of the COMMON GOOD recognized as sacred.

This search for the COMMON GOOD of men furthers the growth of CHRIST in me and in others.

This growth of CHRIST in me and in others is the only assurance of my own perfection.

Thanks to CHRIST, Son of God and Son of man, I can be attentive to the word of God that other men are for me.

Thus can be restored in me the purity of my original nature. In conforming myself to CHRIST I become what in the depths of myself, in the truth of my being created by God I am with other men —a member and a living cell of the TOTAL CHRIST.

This direction of thought prepares man to enter into the mystery of the CHURCH.

PART THREE
The Times We Live In

I

By Faith

"We are the true sons of Abraham, on the march
through the desert of this life toward the promised
land."

Francis of Assisi

"BY FAITH . . ." (Heb. 11).

A. The FAITH of Abraham: He believed the word of God. In the 12th chapter of Genesis God calls Abraham: "Now the Lord said to Abram, 'Go from your country and your kindred and your father's house to the land that I will show you. And I will make of you a great nation, and I will bless you and make your name great, so that you will be a blessing. . . .' So Abram went as the Lord had told him" (Gen. 12, 1-4).

Abraham is our father in the FAITH as we say in the Canon of the Mass. He believed. "He went out," the author of the Epistle to the Hebrews underlines with insistence, "not knowing where he was to go" (Heb. 11, 8). The FAITH of Abraham lies not so much in his leaving his father and mother, relatives and friends, but in his leaving on the word of God without knowing where he was going toward a land of which God only says that it is a "land that I will show you." (Note the future tense.)

We can imagine the vision of the future that pervaded the dreams of Abraham as he advanced slowly at the head of his world of animals and people to the West toward the land of Canaan. He dreams of herds of cattle, of sons, and perhaps of a powerful kingdom. "By you all the families of the earth shall bless themselves" (Gen. 12, 3).

109

Morally, Abraham is assuredly not a perfect example of human rectitude. To extricate himself from difficult situations (cf. Gen. 12, 2-23), he uses methods that are not exactly upright. He is primitive and sometimes a bit of a barbarian, but he believes, he confides without reservation in the promise that God has given him; he believes he will inherit a land and a descendance.

Above all, Abraham manifests his FAITH in this expectation of a descendant. He has a son by Hagar his servant but only to satisfy his wife, Sarah, who despairs at remaining childless; it is not to help the Lord to keep his promise. Afterwards, he will become attached to Ishmael, but he will never cease to believe that God is capable of giving him a descendant born of Sarah.

"He did not weaken in FAITH," writes St. Paul to the Romans, "when he considered his own body which was as good as dead because he was about a hundred years old, or when he considered the barrenness of Sarah's womb. No distrust made him waver concerning the promise of God, but he grew strong in his FAITH." (Rom. 4, 19.20).

Of this FAITH Abraham testifies to the extreme limit when on orders from God he shows himself ready to sacrifice Isaac, the son who had at last come into the world and was now a youth. The story as told in Genesis (cf. chapter 22) is moving in its simplicity as it describes the scene: "Abram rose early . . ." The author of the Epistle to the Hebrews insists on the scope of this act of obedience.

"By FAITH Abraham when he was tested, offered up Isaac and he who had received the promises was ready to offer up his only son of whom it was said, 'Through Isaac shall your descendants be named.' He considered that God was able to raise men even from the dead . . ." (Heb.11, 17-19).

Such was the conduct of Abraham, "in hope he believed against hope . . ." (Rom. 4, 18). By his conduct, he is the father of all those who following him will expect the full accomplishment of divine promises.

B. The FAITH of the descendants of Abraham and its final outcome.

In the divine promises, there was also the promise of a land, "the land . . . I will give to you" (Gen. 13, 14. 19).

As a matter of fact, Abraham lived as a stranger in this land, "beneath a tent." His only possession there was the grotto of Machpelah, which he purchased at the price of money for a tomb (cf. Gen. 23). His sons, the patriarchs, will have to wait for centuries before the promise of God is fulfilled.

Finally, with Moses and Joshua, the promise is fulfilled, and the twelve tribes born of Jacob settle in the land of Canaan. But this settlement is far from fulfilling the promise. For from now on, Israel will know constantly recurring wars both against the former occupants of the land and neighboring tribes. After a brief period of splendor and glory under the reign of Solomon, there will be new trials. Schism, civil wars, deportations, exile, and finally successive colonizations by the Assyrians, the Egyptians, the Persians, the Macedonians, the Greeks, and the Romans.

Such a brutal context gives full value to the uninterrupted chain of witnesses who as sons of Abraham have waited firmly for the accomplishment of the divine promises. "These all died in faith not having received what was promised, but having seen it and greeted it from afar" (Heb. 11, 13).

From this painful experience, Israel learns little by little the precarious nature of the material goods with which its ancestors were enchanted and understands that these are only shadows and images. Beyond the shadows and the images, the eyes of the sons of Abraham begin to perceive the real object of God's promise, a "city which has foundations, whose builder and maker is God" (Heb. 11, 10).

Of course, not all the sons of Abraham were conscious of this. The masses continued to cling to the immediate and temporal meaning of the divine promises. "A land and flocks, a race and a kingdom, a temple and a cult . . ." But the heart of Israel lifting itself above these earthly ambitions is henceforth expecting far higher realities, namely, the invisible and eternal realities of God.

The history of Israel thus appears to be a long and necessary succession of painful marches through which the FAITH of Abraham progressively becomes the FAITH of the Virgin Mary.

"Abraham believed God," writes St. Paul, "and it was reckoned to him as righteousness" (Gal. 3, 6). "And blessed is she who believed . . ." says Elizabeth to Mary (Lk. 1, 45).

Through the FAITH of Mary who inherited the FAITH of her ancestors, Christ came into the world. The promises were fulfilled.

The descendants of Abraham according to the flesh en route to the West toward a land of pastures and cattle are replaced by the descendants of Abraham according to the Spirit (cf. Gal. 3, 29; 4, 21. 29). Those en route to the East to the total Christ will find their eternal country in the Church, and they will be the flock of the eternal shepherd.

C. Evolution of the FAITH in the expression given to it by each man in the passage of time.   The history of Israel foreshadows the history each Christian must live in his personal, inner experience. It is also the figure of the history all Christians must live collectively through the vicissitudes that the Church encounters here below.

The object of our FAITH is always the same. It is the word of God; that is, it is definitively God himself. But its expression will be necessarily tied to the level of understanding men have of the plan of God.

The stages through which the FAITH of Abraham became the FAITH of the Virgin tell us that time is necessary for FAITH to become truly perfect in us. They also tell us that we will perhaps undergo many a heartbreak before the veil of perishable and visible realities is lifted from our eyes. Our hearts need to be remade, and for that they must first be crushed by existence before they can find themselves capable of discerning and desiring the invisible and eternal realities to which God invites us (cf. 2 Cor. 3, 4). In the course of this journey, our faith will have found different expressions throughout our lives.

These demands of faith are to be found as much in the lives of individuals as in collective situations. Thus, on the individual level, the FAITH of a child who in his cradle dreams of a sky filled with the rustle of angels' wings. His FAITH is true, and this expression of this FAITH is real for the child. For an adult, this expression of FAITH would be dangerous and childish as was the FAITH of the Jews who laid claim to Abraham and Moses to refuse the message of Paul after they had refused the testimony of Christ. How many detachments lie between the true FAITH of the little child and the true FAITH of the real adult!

This example of an individual situation may allow us to understand an example taken from the life of the Church.

The crusaders who answered the call of the popes and went to battle shouting, "It is the will of God," journeyed to Palestine to free the tomb of Christ. Frankish barons, slayers of Moor and Saracen, the Knights of St. John, the Knights of Rhodes and those of Malta, sea wolves pitted against the Barbary pirates—all had the true faith. But were a modern Christian to express his faith similarly, it would be fatal not only to his adversaries but also to his own personal faith. What would remain of his faith in a God of love?

From these examples we can better understand what must be our fidelity of attention to the word of God that is time, whether it be our own personal age or the period of time which God has chosen for him to live.

To reach the perfection of FAITH, we must advance in existence without letting ourselves be hindered by the outward forms in which FAITH has expressed itself—whether in our own time or in the course of the centuries that have preceded us. This implies close attention to the message of time.

Conclusions: Listening to time, the Christian advances in FAITH.
Whoever knows how to listen to the call of time will advance in FAITH. He will neither deny nor despise any of the previous expressions of FAITH. He will know how to appreciate them, to admire them to the degree that they are authentic, whether they occurred in his own life when he was younger (in his own childhood piety for example), or were elaborated in the past or in regions or countries of different cultures. But he will never try to revive these expressions of FAITH, or to transplant them, even less will he try to keep them alive. Attention to time will keep him in touch with reality, in association with the vital forces of the present. As much for his own personal use as for that of the generation to which he belongs, he will know how to lend himself to the elaboration of new outward forms in which these vital forces demand to express FAITH in the Living God, who spoke to Abraham.

"No one showed me what I ought to do," wrote Francis of Assisi, the Poverello, in his *Testament*. He reminds us in this phrase that he refused systematically to borrow his religious inspiration from the monastic tradition of past centuries, for his purpose was to reply to a personal aspiration in which an expectation contemporary to his own times was expressed. To advance in FAITH is nothing else but this.

FIRST REFLECTION ON THE THEME
By Faith

A. POINTS FOR MEDITATION

1. The value of a man's FAITH is manifested by his availability ever to go beyond himself according to the demands of life.

2. It is not a proof of the authenticity of one's FAITH to despise in others the expressions of a religious life that we once called our own.

3. Israel purified the eyes of its FAITH only following a collective enterprise of reflection to which many generations were associated. The Christian, when he reaches a purification of the expression of his FAITH, is always the beneficiary of the progress made by his predecessors and his contemporaries.

4. He who believes that he can pride himself on the authenticity of his FAITH is all the more obliged to consider himself accountable for this good to the FAITH of the entire Church.

5. To be attentive to the vital forces for the moment does not mean to seek exclusively the clients and jobs that are profitable. It is to be attentive to all the currents in which the real life of men expresses itself.

6. Economical and technical realities are those that mark modern man the most deeply. FAITH will consist in discerning how these realities can convey the Kingdom for us. We can then bring the vital forces of the moment into submission to the action of the Lord.

7. There can be no opposition between the laws governing the physical universe and those that direct the moral world. These two worlds are one whose author is God. FAITH in this God will therefore manifest itself also in the reception given to every discovery of the laws of the physical world, especially in the technological and

scientific domain, where rigorous methods guarantee the authenticity of the results. To welcome these results with confidence is one of the modern expressions of FAITH.

8. The outcry of workers and the convulsions it produces in economic and social life is easily a cause of scandal for the man who is above all preoccupied with the requirements of law and order. Do we see sufficiently in a strike, beyond demands for wages, the expression of a need for dignity in which rebellious man testifies that he feels and wills himself to be a son of God?

"STRONG IN HIS FAITH" (cf. Rom. 4, 20)

A. Evolution of FAITH in the forms that express it during the course of time. The history of Israel shows us the same FAITH in the same God lived in a totally different manner by the first descendants of Abraham and by the immediate ancestors of the Virgin Mary.

The movement that carried Israel from the FAITH of Abraham to the FAITH of Mary must be relived in each Christian destiny. An exigency of going ever beyond oneself works inside of each one of the baptized (and in the world of the baptized). Gradually, certain principles of action or practical attitudes that formerly received wide acceptance are eliminated because they are foreign and even inimical to the faith. Such is the case in the matter of slavery. Admittedly, it was no problem for St. Paul (cf. 1 Tim. 6; Eph. 6, 5-9; Col. 3, 22.25), the contemporary Christian conscience finds it contrary to the Gospel, and this because of the centuries of maturation that have preceded him and because he lives in a renewed economic context.

This example lived by the Church allows us to understand in what attention to time consists, for we see to what a transformation this attention can lead. It is the same in our personal lives. The elements of our personalities have been taken from the world of time (atavism, environment, habits). Our weakness consists in giving an eternal value to these elements gathered from time. We do this whenever we make an absolute out of some point of view or form of life in which our personalities have found the easiest way to express themselves.

We testify to this by our lack of humility in the sense that humility is the profound conscience of our true condition which is literally a condition of earthliness, a condition of "becoming," a situation in one moment of time. Young and old are equally exposed to this lack of humility. The old give an absolute value to that which has always been done, the young think it an absolute obligation to promote everything that is new.

Thus, in the name of the same FAITH men confront each other because they do not know how to remain deeply attentive to the message of their time.

In their confrontations with each other, men give a permanent value to the realities that are dear to them. The most convenient argument is then to invoke in favor of the reality that one cherishes the guarantee of a miracle, or the results obtained in the present and in the past.

Scripture tells us that in the course of its history, Israel had to detach itself from many of the realities that had received the guarantee of a miracle from God—its national territory, Jerusalem, and the Temple. This is evident proof that the miracles that assured the conquest saved Jerusalem from siege (2 Chr. 32, 20. 23) and consecrated the Temple through fire from heaven (2 Chr. 5, 11. 14) had been momentary guarantees corresponding to a well determined stage in the evolution of the FAITH of the people born of Abraham.

B. FAITH and improvement to be accomplished in the life of the entire Church. This teaching of the scriptures makes us understand how the tendency to gain inspiration oneself systematically from the expressions that FAITH has given of itself in the past can be fatal to true FAITH.

FAITH is "total risk" run by reliance on the word of God.

"Abraham left. . . ." FAITH is expressed in the person who runs this risk. It will necessarily take on the characteristics of the period of economic evolution, and of cultural, psychological and social development as lived by a person (or a group) at a given moment.

At its most rudimentary level, FAITH expresses itself through images. Eternal death has been expressed by medieval man in images of deviltries. As for eternal life, it has been reserved to the theologians to give us an expression for it—the vision of God. Of these two images the first is inherited from a primitive mentality and makes the word, "hell," intolerable to the conscience of evolved man. The second image, inherited from the Greek philosophers, wearies the

technological man of the western world. The last ends are deval-
uated because we have not known how to reinvent the parables
out of the culture that is proper to our own time (cf. Mt. 13, 34).

On a level more intellectual than that of images are formal statements.

God in the scriptures has not given us a collection of formal statements; he has given us the secret of his presence in our lives. It was
therefore necessary for us to elaborate formal statements which, to
understand them, really requires a special education; they are marked
by a certain sophistication. To give them more importance than the
scriptures is to dam up the flow of God's gifts and to reserve the right
to enjoy them to the privileged (cf. Mt. 23, 13).

On its most concrete level FAITH finds its expression in gestures,
attitudes, and customs.

All our lives are made up of the gestures and attitudes that express us through the environment in which we have lived. Through
personal attachment on account of habits bound up with our education or perhaps out of sentimentality, we impose these expressions
on other men. Now for them, these expressions have no link with
their real lives. Even at the cost of tremendous sacrifices in men and
material this evangelization would end in failure (cf. Gal. 6, 7.8).
Proof of this has been seen on the environmental level as well as on
the level of peoples and civilizations.

True FAITH is capable of going beyond images, formal statements, usage and custom to remain attentive to the vital forces of
the moment. These forces will express in their own original forms
the total risk that men run by their reliance on the word of God
heard at a precise moment of time (cf. Lk. 5, 5).

The human groups that claim to live according to FAITH must
be aware that their existence is conditioned by the response their
members give to the summons of time.

This should be of particular concern to religious communities and
to the clerical body. The crisis of vocations, before calling for a
renewal in methods of recruitment, calls for a renewal, through
attention to time, of all that henceforth is no longer an authentic expression of FAITH. To ignore this in the name of sacred fidelities

is to refuse the promptings of the Holy Spirit. To back up this refusal
by recalling miracles of the past is to renew the error and the fault of
Israel according to the flesh. One has then ceased to live by faith.

C. FAITH and improvement to be accomplished in the personal life of the Christian who is seeking life.

The same reflections find their application on the level of personal life.

From a childish FAITH correctly nourished with images spontaneously open to the awesome, we must enter a FAITH purified
of every trace of a childish or adolescent mentality, the faith of an
adult who has come to give the object of his faith its real characteristics to those of God.

When God calls a man, he calls him just as he is. Of course, God
invites us to his life, but he takes into account our aptitude to represent this life to ourselves, and makes us desire it in ways that appear
desirable to us. To Abraham he promised land, herds of cattle, and
children. What could be more desirable for a nomadic shepherd?

This brings us back to all the great desires that may have formed
themselves in our hearts. All these "mad" dreams were calls from
God. Of these dreams, nothing perhaps will be accomplished according to the letter. But for him who has allowed life to purify his
dreams, the reality, from step to step, will surpass everything that
was expressed in them by his legitimate desires.

It is certain that God will fulfill our expectations.

"Fear not," he said to Abraham who was beginning to find the
delay too long, "I am your shield. Your reward shall be very great."

But it is just as certain that our dreams will have to be left behind,
for we must not confuse God with the various human and personal
attractions with which he will have clothed himself to make himself desired by us. This requires of us that we are willing in advance
through FAITH to be attentive to time. We must be docile enough
to be able to detach ourselves from everything and everyone in which
and in whom we have believed in order to believe only in him.

In one's personal life as in the life of the Church, there are many
images from which we must be detached. We would have to detach
ourselves from them even if they had come directly from God with
the surety of a miracle to back them up.

In the past, so-called experts on the spiritual life wrote a number of treatises on Christian perfection for other Christians who wanted to become holy. As time went on, however, these writings became more and more stylized conglomerations of all the characteristics, practices, and virtues of the saints of the 18th and 19th centuries. They undoubtedly thought that by writing these treatises they would help other Christians. What they produced, however, was insubstantial.

Today, we look back on all this and wonder how we can possibly reproduce in our own lives the pious practices, and virtues of the martyrs, virgins, widows, and confessors who have preceded us in the history of the Church. It is interesting to note that St. Theresa of Lisieux, perhaps one of the greatest saints of all time, refused to draw her inspirations from any of the stylized portrayals of the saints. "I am too little," she said.

We know how Pius XI enthusiastically received her writings. He referred to her as the "cherished child of the whole world." But have we really understood that this was in fact a sigh of relief?

A half century after Theresa wrote her *The Story of a Soul,* there are still many people who thirst for God, but who are hampered by spiritual directors who rely too heavily for them on the classic approaches to sanctity. Many a David cannot advance because the armor a Saul has clotherd him with makes it impossible (cf. 1 Sam. 17, 38).

The perfection to which God calls us cannot be stylized. We advance toward it to the degree that we answer the calls that come to us in the voices of our personal nature, our fellowmen, and the times in which we live.

Conclusions: Adaptability in FAITH and the power of Christ in us. The present time, characterized by the rapid rhythm of the transformation of forms of life, will certainly give FAITH expressions whose outward traits will be less easy to catalog than in the past. Christian life and its perfection will simply adopt the features of the situation in which each one will have to live. There will still be the necessity of detaching oneself from these as soon as they in turn express only past realities. This disengagement will be the guarantee of the authenticity of FAITH in each one. It will be ordinary and at the same time demanding.

Francis of Assisi was, in his times, a perfect example of this ability to surpass what is outmoded. He was able to pass from the ideal of a soldier of the commune of Assisi at the battle of St. John's Bridge to the ambition of becoming famous at the service of the Italian cause under the protection of the Pope, then to the work of restoring churches and chapels, and from there-to the ideal of caring for the members of Christ among the lepers. Finally, he came to the simple idea of leading a life that would be such that by this life alone the Good News would be proclaimed.

The Poverello did not allow himself to be stopped at any one of these successive stages; he *passed* through all of them even when God had given to one or the other of them the surety of a miracle. After passing through them, he never denied or disavowed the past. Faith had made him a true son of Abraham.

"He grew strong in his FAITH," wrote St. Paul speaking of Abraham (Rom. 4, 20).

Faith fills the baptized with the power of Christ to bring humanity, for which he is responsible, to salvation and to lead himself as well, a member of the body of Christ, to perfection.

SECOND REFLECTION ON THE THEME
By Faith

A. POINTS FOR MEDITATION

1. The judgment that God will bring to bear on each man will not be a sifting through of all the actions he has performed in his life but the revelation of the self-accomplishment each one will have reached in the context of his own life (cf. 2 Cor. 5, 10).

2. To fulfill oneself is not to realize a program of personal perfection the characteristics of which are determined in advance. We fulfill ourselves through willing to be that which the providential context of our life (family, environment, period of time) can elaborate in us if we open ourselves to it totally.

3. To live thus, willing ourselves to be faithful to the truth within the historic development of our existence here below, is to live ac-

cording to FAITH. He who lives according to FAITH testifies to his
certitude that God, who gave his Son so that the world would not
perish, loves his own creation in man sufficiently to give it everything required for its full achievement (cf. Rom. 8, 29. 32).

4. To be perfect is not to achieve in ourselves an individual or
collective image corresponding to a standard model (cf. Mt. 19, 21).
Perfection here below can only be the perfection of our FAITH expressing itself in a corresponding praxis (cf. Gal. 5, 6).

On the individual level, this praxis will develop following the
rhythm of experiences already lived. Each one of the ages of life
expresses in its own way FAITH in the living God. Patience in the
acceptance of the stages that others are going through is the most
reliable criterion of the authenticity of the FAITH on which one
prides oneself. On the collective level, this praxis will differ according
to time and place. Environment (racial, cultural, social) must express, in their own way FAITH in the God who possesses all things.
Not to accept this fact would testify to personal weakness in FAITH.

5. Whether it be on a personal or a collective level, to live according to FAITH necessarily leads man to lead himself at all times in
the direction of the truth, however cruel may be the detachments
which he senses will accompany this *engagement*. In his fidelity to
advance according to the truth that reveals itself to him, man obeys
God, and his attitude of obedience makes him capable of doing
whatever God asks of him (cf. Rom. 4, 20-21).

B. PARTICULAR THEMES;

Priests. Do we show to higher authority as much docility as we
expect from those who are subject to us? Do we have toward those
who are subject to us as much open-mindedness and receptivity as
we hope to find in our own superiors? Do we obey declarations of
the Church when they are to our advantage and criticize them when
we find that they contradict us.

A form of obedience proper to modern man is to accept new
ways by which we can maintain ourselves on the level of new technological advances and of the evolution of thought. The sons of this
world do this by necessity, for profit motives; the sons of light do it
because they have FAITH.

C. Texts for Reading and Prayer

a. Biblical Texts

The entire **Old** Testament in an expression of the FAITH of Israel. In
particular, read the history of Abraham, Gen. 12—25.

Suggested plan for this reading: chapter 15, material promises; chapters 12 and 20, scenes of a primitive existence; chapter 17, the history of Ishmael. God rejects nothing that man does with rectitude;
chapter 19, the origin attributed to the Moabites is compared; compare the origin attributed to the Moabites with the Book of Ruth;
chapter 22, "It was his only son that he offered." In the Old Testament, compare with the faith of Moses, of Gideon, Jg. 6, 7.8, and
also the Books of Esther, Tobit, Judith, and 1 Maccabees. In the
New Testament, compare Rom. 4, 23; 5, 12; 8, 28-39; Gal. 6, 13-14;
2, 1-4, 10; Eph. 2, 9; Mt. 8, 5-14; 15, 20-29.

b. Prayers

Is. 38, 9-20; Mic. 7, 18-20. Unshakable FAITH in God.
Pss. 13; 16; 27; 33; 56; 62; 73. The entire psalter is a cry of FAITH
by Israel to its God, the living God.

Final Theme

Gal. 2, 20.

II

Thanks to Poverty

"Let (poverty) be your portion for it leads to the
land of the living."

St. Francis of Assisi *Rule, 6.*

BLESSED ARE THE POOR (Mt. 5, 3).

A. Evolution of the Mind of   The essential history of Israel
Israel, from the esteem of   can be summed up in the evolu-
wealth to the acceptance of   tion that led the FAITH of Israel
poverty.   to become the FAITH of the Vir-
gin Mary.

This evolution was a masterpiece of God. But we must not see in
it an almost miraculous accomplishment, dramatic change without
roots in historical reality. It is the normal outcome of the situations
that the people of God had come to know in the course of their
history. It must be related very particularly to the economic context
in which Israel had lived.

It is necessary to note and understand the successive attitudes of
Israel in regard to wealth.

Until the days of the prophets, wealth was considered in Israel to
be a sign of friendship of the Almighty. Abraham (cf. Gen. 13)
and Jacob (cf. Gen. 30) became wealthy. Moses despoiled the Egyptians (cf. Exod. 12, 35). In the days of Joshua and Judges, there was
rapine and pillaging. For the conscience of Israel, all these events
were so many testimonials of divine favor. The sums of gold and
silver left by the dying David to his son, Solomon (cf. 1 Chr. 28, 29)
must be understood in the same fashion. The conclusion of the book

124

of Job (cf. Job 62, 12) testifies to the persistence of this mentality. To be rich was to be blessed by the Lord!

Nevertheless, three centuries after Solomon, a passage from Deuteronomy warns Israel against wealth. The possession of material goods is presented in it as a danger of forgetting God (Deut. 6, 10-19). And to give greater weight to the warning, the sacred author places it on the lips of Moses the prophet who alone spoke to God as one speaks to a friend (cf. Deut. 34, 10).

We have here an indication of an important change of mind. This complete turnabout can be explained.

Since Solomon, Israel had known only successive impoverishments. During the three centuries that had elapsed, there had been the Schism, the ruin of national and religious unity and the destruction of the kingdom of Samaria; now Jerusalem and the kingdom of Judea were threatened. Along Israel's frontiers, there were no longer only restless tribes who were kept at a distance by an occasional thrashing. Powerful empires had been constituted and the People of God cut a rather poor figure beside them (cf. 1 Kgs. 12f. and the entire second Book of Kings). Israel had learned to feel small!

Thus, from Abraham to Solomon, nine centuries of continuous progress had resulted in the fulfillment of a material dream, a kingdom that gathered together the descendants of Abraham under the scepter of Solomon, the son of David, and the builder of the Temple.

After Solomon begins a fresh progression of nine centuries. This second progression will result in the consciousness that the kingdom is a spiritual reality, a kingdom of holiness gathering together the true sons of Abraham under the scepter of the true Prince of Peace, the son of David, builder of the eternal temple that is the Church.

There are first of all three centuries of material losses that deprive Israel of its unity, its independence, and finally, its very existence. With exile, everything is stripped away—lands and houses, vines and fig trees, gold and silver.

But after this will come a deprivation that will be far more difficult to accept. During the course of the six centuries that still separate it from Christ, Israel will have to renounce all the dreams of power and glory revived in its heart by the memories of the reign of Solomon.

B. From the acceptance of ma-   It was not easy for Israel to
   terial poverty to the entry into renounce dreams of power and
   spiritual poverty.   glory. It is even certain that with-
                                         out the material losses and the
state of destruction imposed by the Schism, the loss of independence,
the ruin of Jerusalem and of the Temple, the exile, and the successive
colonizations, Israel would have never been in the frame of mind to
accomplish this decisive step.

But the complete downfall of everything in which the admirers
of Solomon had taken pleasure was for Israel the providential context of life within which its religious conscience was able to revise
the expression of its fidelity to the Lord.

We must represent this revision as spaced out over a whole series
of generations. From father to son, the questioning goes on. In face
of the inexplicable ruin of the dream inherited from Solomon, an
answer had to be found. One facile explanation said that the sins
of Israel had merited these punishments. But then, why did the sons
have to carry the burden of the sins committed by the fathers?
(cf. Ezek. 18)

In this meditation the hope of Israel found its purification, and
admitted the ruin of its dream while continuing to believe firmly
in the fidelity of God to his promises. The heart of Israel understood
that the accomplishment of the promises belonged to the Lord. This
heart of Israel renounced the vision of receiving the reward for its
hope in the following manner. It was satisfied with the thought that
whatever came about, God would certainly fulfill its deepest expectations (Is. 55, 6).

In this frame of mind, Israel tore itself away from everything that
was too human in the dream of its ancestors. Above all the heart
of Israel tore itself away from everything included in this dream that
was impure and even inhuman: its desire for material triumphs, for
bloody victories, for pitiless reprisals, and for gloating vengeance
(cf. Ps. 109; Ps. 137, 8.9).

The renunciation of all this apocalyptic imagery expressed itself
in God's people through the apparition of a new human category,
the poor. The poor are not a social category. Their poverty is not an
economic condition.

They are poor through a deep inclination of their minds and hearts. They expect nothing from the assurances given by human power, they expect everything from the fidelity of the Lord.

These poor are the culmination of a long purification of the hope of Israel. When Christ finally appears, they are present, and because he has encountered them on his way, Christ declares that they are blessed and that "the kingdom of God belongs to them" (Mt. 5, 3). By this declaration, Christ means to say that only dispositions of inner poverty can make man capable of hearing the Good News of the true Kingdom to which God invited man on the day he called Abraham.

This poverty, which makes man capable of hearing the beatitudes proclaimed with their paradoxes and their follies, is, above all, an inner attitude. But the history of Israel will always remind the baptized that this was the slowly ripening fruit of six centuries of reflection coming after three centuries of deprivations.

It is through and also beyond these outward deprivations that the attitude of mind and heart proclaimed by Jesus as an evangelical virtue was elaborated. Material poverty was the catalyst, because of which the hope of Israel was able to evolve from a temporal messianism inherited from the admirers of Solomon to a messianism of holiness, desiring and calling for the true prince of peace. Without the loss of material goods, in which for some time it had seen a sign of divine friendship, Israel would have never had access to the vision (the exact idea) of the spiritual reality that God proposed to establish one day in favor of all men by the coming into the world of his son.

C. Poverty and "Christian hope." On the collective as well as on the individual level, the Christian is the true Israel of God.

The history lived by the people of Israel tells the Christian clearly enough that without poverty, he cannot form the right ideas about the kingdom of holiness of which God has made him the inheritor and the king through his baptism (cf. Rom. 8, 17).

However, the Christian through the interplay of his existence, must still allow the Lord to provide him with the indispensable, exterior deprivations through which dispositions of true poverty may be elaborated in his heart.

On the level of the collective life of the Church, the Lord's solicitude has never failed to manifest itself. It is a sort of law that the goods of the Church, as they increase, finish by requiring of themselves a sort of return to the masses. One wonders, when considering this fact and comparing it to the history of Israel, why certain heads of Churches wear themselves out trying to reconstitute such ephemeral patrimonies.

On the level of individual life the solicitude of the Lord manifests itself in different ways. For some, there is the call to abandon everything they posses. For others there are reversals of fortune that accomplish the same results even if they are less voluntary. For all, there is the series of material deprivations put into motion by entry into adult life. There is the alteration of youth's freshness, the diminution of certain qualities of physical vigor, resistance, and endurance, the progressive appearance of the consequences of aging, the loss of those who aided us at our entry into life, the necessity to be helped, to be cared for, and perhaps one day, the obligation to become totally dependent on others.

It is through these deprivations or more precisely, beyond the condition of impoverishment in which they leave us that gradually we see and allow the formation in ourselves of the deep attitudes of poverty of heart and spirit. How many are there who had thought themselves poor at an early age and who then went on to see later by their lack of disengagement that circumstances revealed in them at the end of their lives how superficial their poverty really was and how tenuous its connection with their inner lives.

When one has reached true dispositions of poverty of heart, he knows how to lose without becoming ill over the loss of many things from which he would never have considered separating himself of his own free will. We allow others to take what we would not have found hard to give them. We accept that a rightful liberty may express itself without our previous consent. We let another have the joy of discovering for himself what we would have loved to teach him.

These different manifestations of an inner frame of mind animated by evangelical poverty allow us to discern what poverty brings to the Christian. It makes him lucid enough to be able to detach himself from the images on which he has lived as those that are left behind and must be replaced by others. Poverty makes possible the purification of hope. It never allows the Christian to become the prisoner of familiar situations and tried methods, of favored techniques, nourished hopes, or desired revenge.

Conclusions: Importance of the virtue of poverty. At all periods of Christian history, we can see Christians substituting the earthly hopes of various messianisms for the hope of the kingdom of holiness. Even so-called religious men, thinking they were serving God, no longer served him, the living God who calls man to his life.

It is, in fact, easy for us frequently to serve a God of our own choices or inventions. From this God, just as Israel according to the flesh, we expect the accomplishment of our plans, our ideas and our dreams. But are we happy even if these plans, ideas, and dreams are only childish and materialistic! For it can happen without our knowing it that they are selfish, unjust, and even inhuman. We have become again despite baptism one of those Hebrews for whom the inventory of the treasures of David and the results of raids carried on in neighboring lands constitute the much appreciated proof of the Lord's benedictions.

Every day a Christian must ask himself, "By what images am I guided? What inner vision occupies my attention?" But these questions only the poor in spirit ask themselves.

Just as it was the catalyst through which Israel passed from a temporal messianism to the messianism of holiness, poverty that is first of all outward deprivation and then a disposition of the heart fosters in each Christian individually and in the Church collectively the purification of hope and the evolution of FAITH that creates true sons of Abraham.

"Cleave to poverty unreservedly . . . for it has made you heirs and kings of the Kingdom of Heaven . . . for it leads to the land of the living," said Francis of Assisi to his brothers. One cannot express this truth more aptly.

FIRST REFLECTION ON THE THEME
Thanks to Poverty

A. POINTS FOR MEDITATION

1. Of the nine centuries from Solomon to Jesus, the first three are a time of exclusively material deprivation. These three centuries were indispensable for the forming in Israel of dispositions of poverty of spirit during the six centuries that followed.

2. To wish to give man the means to desire nothing any more is to destroy him while pretending to satisfy him. That which man needs the most in order to survive is the will to live.

3. The will to live is, first of all, bound up with an intuition that we have of going beyond the present; that there is something more to existence. To claim to establish here below situations that are perfect would be to condemn oneself to destroy his own inherent dynamism.

4. Poverty is an indispensable dimension of the survival of man because to cease to desire is to cease to live.

5. There are ways to give that are the best means of keeping others dependent.

6. To guarantee young people a life to which they have contributed nothing is to condemn them to boredom and finally, to revolt. They do not want to die.

7. It is easier to surround a man with objects than to plunge him into an atmosphere that simulates his will to live. Such an atmosphere will necessarily contain a note of poverty because poverty is a condition of becoming.

8. To live to become is a characteristic of man. Truly human life and therefore Christian life declines when the aspiration toward something else no longer exists.

9. Hope dies as much from the satiety of the unnecessary as through the privation of necessities. Poverty saves hope.

10. Reflection on poverty is one of the major questions of our time. A civilization of abundance can destroy man by glutting him.

"LEARNING FROM GOD"

A. Poverty in the renunciation of material goods and dreams of power. In the course of Israel's history, the law of poverty played first on the material level, then, on the level of the intellect, and finally, in the depths of the heart.

It was hard for Israel to lose its national unity and its independence, soil, and possessions. But without a miracle to deliver it, Israel had to make a virtue of its necessity.

On the other hand, to renounce dreams of power and glory and desire for crushing revenge on the "day of the Lord" was more difficult for Israel, and many never took that step.

This history of Israel repeats itself in many forms throughout the history of each Christian and in the history of the Church, which is to say that poverty of material goods does not necessarily introduce man to poverty of spirit.

On the most material level, this deprivation can constitute simply a Christian variety of falsity. At one period of Church history, those who boasted of it gave themselves the title of "spirituals." They claimed that by their discipline they submitted the flesh to the spirit. The outcome of their adventure proved that only the pride of their spirit found satisfaction in the disciplining of the flesh. The same situation can appear in new forms.

Of course, the incarnation implies a visible, even painful manifestation of poverty, but poverty is evangelical and Christian only when it expresses the renunciation of the support given by human power.

Human power can take on different forms throughout the ages. There is the power of arms and of the iron fist, as well as the power of money and of cunning. And more recently there is the power of the information media. There is also the more dangerous power of manipulating the power of the masses. Evangelical poverty demands that we renounce all of these powers and that we repudiate all the dreams for which they are used.

131

When the time came for Israel to recognize in Christ the accomplishment of the divine promises, the greatest obstacle to its recognition was not the possession of material goods. Lazarus and his friends were wealthy as were Nicodemus and Joseph of Arimethea (cf. Lk. 8, 3).

Its greatest obstacle was the attachment of many Jews to their dreams of power and glory. It was this attachment rather than the possession of material goods that made them incapable of receiving the Good News. This attachment paralyzed them all the more because it was materialized in the cult of determined, outward signs such as race, the Law, and the Temple. This cult made true poverty impossible for them.

B. Poverty in the renunciation of "signs." We must insist here on the fact that the human being in his depths is less attached to things than to what these things mean for him.

In consequence, poverty does not consist in the renunciation of things, but in the detachment from what these things signify.

It can therefore accommodate itself to the use of the most modern technology in the measure that technology frees us. Yet, it can also succumb to attachment to an antique keepsake and becomes paralyzed.

But even more paralyzing than souvenirs and more enslaving than all of modern technology are the ideas that we cherish of the system which we must prove to be the right one, intellectual self-sufficiency, the illusion of knowing everything and that (more serious still) of being the first one to know, the conviction that we come after a generation that was ignorant or incapable, and the will to establish our influence over others. All these make true poverty impossible for the Christian.

Above all, evangelical poverty is impossible, whatever the outward deprivations, wherever there is a craze for signs. This is the case when some are determined to impose on others either outward forms that have had value in the past, or outward forms expressing an interior renewal that does not yet exist in fact. Whether it be attachment to signs that characterized a past that has remained dear to us or attachment to signs that will no doubt express the future, *there is always a refusal of true poverty whenever a man glorifies himself on his fidelity to outward signs.* This refusal of true poverty makes true FAITH impossible, and above all when several people are gathered together in mutual esteem and admiration before their own fidelity to the signs that give them satisfaction. Thus, one "receives glory one from another." "How can you believe who receive glory one from another?" (Jn. 5, 44). Thus spoke Jesus expressing his compassion for those Jews for whom the absence of true poverty was an obstacle to the purification of Israel's hope and its entry into the perfection of FAITH (cf. Acts 28, 20; Heb. 12, 2).

C. True poverty manifests itself through docility to the Holy Spirit who speaks in time. The history of Israel shows therefore that the value of poverty lies entirely in the ability that it established in man in relation to the Spirit of God to going beyond signs.

Victims of their attachment to signs, the Jews, contrary to all the appeals of their own consciences, were able to contemplate the killing of Christ (cf. Jn. 5, 18). When a Christian places his glory in fidelity to signs he can in the name of FAITH come to commit acts that are contrary to the conscience of mankind as a whole. He too "kills Christ" because in the name of his attachments he empties Christ out of his own life and the lives of his fellowmen. It is the tragic mistake, often renewed in the Christian's past in the name of the Christ of our choice of killing the Christ image of God (cf. 2, Cor. 4, 3. 7; Gal. 6, 12-15). Only true poverty can spare human fidelities—and the will to fidelity—from this error.

Thus, even a situation of real poverty is subject to caution if this situation is to be used as a base or staging area for influence on others instead of being used as a support for a more total availability to others.

True poverty makes man capable of being taught. By making him ready to be on the march, it prepares him to be able to go beyond himself according to the invitations of God at each stage of the road. It makes a man capable of hearing the summons of his own times.

At an hour when God wishes to bring about the renewal of his Church, poverty thus understood is the great virtue, the great opportunity to be of use. It is poverty which at this time creates the right

climate for relations between Christian confessions and allows them
to encounter each other. It is poverty which beyond the hoped for
unity of Christian confessions could bring the expression of universal
FAITH to such a degree of purity that unbelievers themselves
would have no difficulty in recognizing in it the manifestation of the
truth sought by every human conscience (2 Cor. 4, 2).

It remains to be said what "poverty" is. Perhaps this is impossible
because in reality poverty is nothing.

The history of Israel makes poverty appear as a catalyst. In a
chemical reaction, the catalyst does not become part of the process,
but only makes it possible. Without it, the reaction would not occur.

It is the same with poverty. It is not a state of life nor an intellectual choice, even less is it a slogan or banner. It is nothing that can be
defined. Nonetheless, without it, there are processes that are not
initiated and there are obstructions that do occur.

Poverty is like life. One cannot define it or isolate it. It just is.
And where it is, it reveals its presence without words through its
effects and its fruits.

One cannot define life, but it is possible to describe living. One
cannot define poverty but one can describe the poor. The poor man
is he who after accepting himself and after having accepted others
and his own times, will, in this forsaking any right to direct the
course of history, has known how to let the "Spirit of the Lord act
in him" (St. Francis *Rule,* 10). He keeps himself unattached and free
to reply to every appeal that comes to him from life.

Conclusions: The meaning of poverty and appreciation of Scripture.

Poverty is therefore an incom-
parable wealth and at the same
time, not something that man can
acquire once and for all.

One can even have had it for a time and then have lost it. The
meaning of poverty is kept intact in the heart of man only through
applied meditation of Scripture. Without ceasing, we must rethink
the lesson that is represented by the reversal of Israel for the accomplishment of which nine centuries of deprivations were not enough.

Without any distinction of philosophies or religions, St. Francis of
Assisi is recognized as the living incarnation of perfect poverty. He
had found the meaning of poverty in Scripture. When he speaks
of poverty, his language is scriptural in its vocabulary and in its

images. For him the bible, as much in the Old Testament as in the New, is the first "apology for the Poor," the true poor, an apology that was lived. All the illusions on the subject of poverty are denounced in the bible. They are denounced at the very point to which the purification of Israel's hope leads, and which is the perfect expression of its FAITH. This point is the heart of the Virgin, the poorest of the poor, who expects the Word of God, and is made fruitful by that Word.

The purity of consent that a human being will thus give to situations that existence brings about for him is the only thing that allows us to recognize whether he knows the meaning of true poverty which leads to the land of the living.

SECOND REFLECTION ON THE THEME
Thanks to Poverty

A. POINTS FOR MEDITATION

1. Life situations, however successful they may be, must never be regarded as final destinations or definitive states of affairs. However good they may be, they become dangerous as soon as they cease to be anything but mere staging areas, points of departure to be left behind by new accomplishments.

2. The excellence and perfection of a life situation, if man becomes enchanted with it, imprisons him without his knowing it in images that express this situation. Man then becomes incapable of progress by his very success; he will live only on his past and regard it as criminal when others refuse to allow themselves to be reduced to it.

3. If the excellence of a real life situation is in the religious order, the danger presented by success is even greater. We are exposed to reducing the KINGDOM of God to a momentary achievement. One can then, in the name of alleged theological principles ruin FAITH in the living God in one's own personal life and, more than one is aware of it, in the collective life of men.

It is most important to note that the preceding truths are usually understood by each of us only in their application to our neighbor. A human being can only feel himself concerned by these truths in the measure that he is animated by a true spirit of poverty.

4. He is poor who at the same time that he grasps and appreciates the deep values of the present moment also discerns their fundamental precariousness with enough lucidity to be able to attach himself to what is of definitive value in them. This capacity for discernment is the mark of the spirit of poverty.

5. Poverty makes us lucid as to the true value of life situations. It makes a man open to any lack of transparence that can put a screen between the aspirations of his heart and God who is its only sufficient end.

6. Poverty makes us free in regard to reality. It makes a man sensitive to every incipient paralysis that comes from an undue attachment to the appearance of things, situations, and persons.

7. Poverty makes us free to rid ourselves of the images that others have already lived, in proportion as these images are passed by and must be replaced with others. Thus does poverty save dynamism of being, possibilities of self-renewal, and youth of mind and body. For the Christian, it is the condition of authentic HOPE.

B. Texts for Reading and Prayer

a. Biblical Texts

Deut. 6, 11. 32. First praise of poverty in the Church.
Is. 9, 7—10, 5. Inevitable blindness of the man who attaches himself to the visible.
Is. 21, 1-15; 61, 8—62, 10. The crushing defeats of Israel prepare it to understand the ways of God. Compare Is. 54; 55; Bar. 4, 5-8, 9; Heb. 11; 12.
Hag. 2, 1-10. The poverty of the new Temple prepares Israel to understand the new relationship that God intends to establish with it. Compare Zech. 9.
Jn. 5, 44. The Jews, enchanted with their dreams (the race, the Law, the Temple), make themselves incapable of recognizing the Son.
Lk. 16, 19-27. Because he was rich, this man had not even seen Lazarus.
Jas. 2 1-10. Respect for the poor.

b. Books

St. Francis, *Rule 11*, chap. 6; *Testament*, 14-27; *Admonitions*.

c. Prayers

Is. 26, 7-20. Instructed by poverty, Israel calls out to God.

The Psalter is full of cries of the poor. Compare Pss. 16; 22; 49; 86; 116; 123; 127; 142; 146.

Mt. 11, 25-30. The most beautiful prayer of the poor.

Final Theme

Lk. 1, 53.

III

Living the Mystery of the Church

"And we were simple and subject to all."
St. Francis, *Testament*

"THE LORD IS IN THIS PLACE"

A. The universal presence of God in the universe is revealed to man. Chapter 28 of the book of Genesis tells us a well known episode in the life of Jacob. The future patriarch, having obtained the paternal blessing through deception fled to the land of Haran. It was better for him not to expose himself to the vengeance of his brother, Esau. One night during the course of this hasty departure Jacob had a dream. He saw, pushed into the earth at the very place where he was resting, a ladder whose summit reached the sky, and on it he saw angels going up and down. There the Lord appeared to him and spoke with him. Jacob, awoke from his sleep and said, "Surely the Lord is in this place and I did not know it." And he was afraid and he said, "How awesome is this place! This is none other than the house of God, and this is the gate of heaven" (Gen. 28, 16).

Let us note well the confession of Jacob, "Surely the Lord is in this place and I did not know it!"

As soon as the first glimmers of conscious life have manifested themselves in a being of flesh and blood, he renders homage to a superior being. Religion and man appeared simultaneously on the earth.

To cultivate the good graces of the superior being that their conscience had glimpsed (cf. Rom. 2, 14) men invented cults. They reserved objects and places for the divinity; these were altars and edifices. As he evolved, religious man consecrated these reserved

138

places (cf. Gen. 28, 18). Through this gesture of consecration, men intended to assure for themselves in a given place the presence of the superior being whose existence was revealed to them by the universe (cf. Rom. 19, 20).

Today, the Church still consecrates edifices.

Following the words of Jesus to the Samaritan woman (cf. Jn. 4, 21) and the discourse of the apostle Paul to the Athenians (cf. Acts 17, 24), this practice of the Church should not surprise us. It should be, on the contrary, a matter for reflection.

Indeed, in the office for the consecration of buildings of worship, the Church repeats like a refrain the words of Jacob, "The Lord is in this place and I did not know it."

By placing on our lips these words that are a confession the Church educates our religious conscience. She teaches us that the rites of the consecration do not make God present; God is already present. The dedication only reveals this presence and brings man to say "The Lord is in this place and I did not know it."

B. Revelation made to us of God's plan that God, present in the world, is pursuing in it. "I did not know it . . ." During his sleep, Jacob had seen; when he awoke he admitted that he had been in ignorance of a secret reality.

Here again, Jacob (Israel) is the image of man. Man has always had the idea of the existence of God, of his power that maintains all things in being, of his majesty that fills all things.

But no man could have had of himself the idea of the presence of God in the created universe, the presence of God by which God is personally engaged in the destiny of his own work. This presence is a secret that spirits themselves could neither guess nor foresee. And how much more so is it beyond human intelligence!

The secret of a seed planted in the soil is revealed only on the day when this seed has become a leafy stem and is able to be identified.

It is the same with the secret of history. The presence of the living God at the heart of his work and the meaning of this presence have been finally revealed to angels as well as to men only through the features assumed by God in the face of Christ Jesus (cf. 2 Cor. 3, 18; 4, 6). Only this coming of Christ into the world has allowed the spirits (principalities and powers, cherubims and seraphims) to enter the knowledge of the mystery of which the created universe was in a way in parturition (cf. Eph. 1, 9; Rom. 8, 22). On the day when Christ appeared, definitely transfigured by the resurrection, both angelic spirit and human intellect could have made their own the confession of Jacob, "surely the Lord is in this place and I did not know it."

The risen Christ reveals to me the presence of God personally engaged in the course of history. He teaches us that the ultimate reality of history is the mysterious action that is accomplished in it. An exchange is taking place. For thousands of years, an incessant current of exchanges is going on between the God who created the universe and the universe that issues from this creative act (cf. Gen. 28, 12). This current of exchanges elaborates a new reality. God is at work inside the universe that he makes fruitful. And from the works of God a new being is born into the universe. Issued from the world created by God, this new being will participate in the uncreated nature of God (2 Pet. 1, 4; 2 Cor. 5, 17; Gal. 6, 15; Col. 2, 17).

This new being has been manifested to men in the person of the risen Christ. In the person of all those who claim to belong to Christ, this new being continues to elaborate itself. Christ is the final outcome of the past, the reason for the present, the finality of all becoming. In Christ, the secret of history is revealed to us; we know the meaning of time; "it is a house of God, the gate of heaven."

C. Man associated with God in the accomplishment of God's plan.

With the coming into the world of the human being, nature has, in a certain way, attained the ultimate expression of itself. Man is at the term of the upsurge of the whole universe. A microcosm, he is, at once, the summing up and the extreme summit of creation.

After the coming of man, all this momentum, as a rocket that has spent itself could only end by falling back. But God, who had foreseen this falling back, assumes the momentum of the universe at its extreme summit which is man. He causes man to enter divine life. He crowns the dynamism of creation by making its highest part enter

incorruptible life. Divine condescendence goes forth to meet the
momentum of the universe. By this free gift, God makes humanity
the first fruits of his work (Jas. 1, 18).

One reservation only: It depends on man to give himself to the
accomplishment of this plan.

On the expanding energies of nature, God had imposed his plan;
from man, who is conscious and free, God asks for consent and
cooperation. After centuries of slow preparation when the fullness of
time had come, God revealed to man in the face of Christ Jesus the
new horizons that were to be reached. Man thus knows how he should
behave in the universe. History appears to him as a becoming to be
accomplished in cooperation with God. Whether it concern his own
personal existence or the destiny of all humanity, man knows that
he advances into his own destiny as in a temple, a sacred place, because he knows henceforth that he is himself a house of God, a temple of the living God (cf. 1 Tim. 3, 15. 16; Heb. 3, 6).

In the measure that the human being, enlightened on his own
destiny through this revelation lends itself to the accomplishment of
God's plan, the exchange between nature and grace follows its
course. From this exchange between a dynamism sprung from below
and grace flowing from above is elaborated in time the eternal masterpiece of God. The total Christ is born of the womb of the universe
just as Christ, the head of the body was born of the womb of the
Virgin, through the operation of the Spirit. In this total Christ nature
and grace will perpetuate their alliance.

In the wonder of the recognition of this effusion of divine life received in the person of Jesus, the entire universe, through the voice
of man, makes its thanksgiving rise toward the Father by chanting
the words of the Psalm: "thou annointest my head with oil"
(Ps. 23, 22). The head is Christ, in whom humanity receives the
unction of divinity (cf. Ps. 45, 8).

In the risen Christ, humanity has ceased to fear death. "Even
though I walk through the valley of the shadow of death, I fear no
evil." It enters a happiness that passes all its expectations. "My cup
overflows." It attains the incorruptibility of glory. "I shall dwell
in the house of the Lord forever."

Conclusions: The authentic mean- This is the revelation that has
ing of the mystery of history been made to us.
makes man free to be moved According to the words of St.
by the action of the Holy Spirit. Paul, "Christ has removed the
veil" (2 Cor. 3, 16). Like Jacob,
humanity in its night here below has had the vision of a ladder planted
in the earth and reaching the depths of the sky. From now on in the
face of every situation that life brings with it in the course of centuries, man knows that the Lord is there. The world, the universe, the
course of history is seen as "a house of God, the gate of heaven and
surely the Lord is in this place."

This revelation completely changes the religious attitude of man.
There can no longer be question of making God present to the world
or of consecrating the world to God by erecting in it gigantic statues,
cathedrals, or obelisks.

The meaning of history is simply that of a dedication ceremony.
But this dedication is not our work and does not belong to us. It is
taking its course and is the work of the Spirit. We do not conduct it;
we are its object. Our part is to give ourselves to it (ecclesial life),
to communicate the Good News to others (evangelization), and to
make them participants in the measure that God has given us the
power and the mandate to do so (sacraments). This role has nothing
to do with a mission to conquer the world and to convert men. For
as much as we must pray and desire the conversion of all to the Lord,
just as much must we be wary of the urge that sometimes makes us
want to convert and to conquer others. This impulse may be expressing only our selfish need to annex others to those structures that create
our own security. This impulse will then subtract us from the action
of the Spirit. We are no longer apt to be moved by the Spirit because,
perhaps without our knowing it, we are ambitious to govern others.

"We should never desire to be above others," writes St. Francis
of Assisi in a letter addressed to all the faithful, "but we ought
rather to be servants and subject to every human creature for God's
sake. And the Spirit of the Lord shall rest upon all those who do
these things and who shall persevere to the end and he shall make
his abode and dwelling in them" (*Letter I*).

His authentic feeling for the mystery of history had made Francis
subject to every creature; he knelt before the priest who was a for-

nicator, gratefully accepted the remonstrances of the peasant of Alverno, and showed his deferential respect to the Sultan.

Perhaps we should see here more than in any other thing the secret of the extraordinary influence that the Poverello has exercised and still exercises on the course of history. Lending himself totally to the action of the Holy Spirit in the universe, he has more than any other man contributed to the elaboration of the new being that is forming itself in the midst of men's lives. And the universe is grateful to him for having lived so truly the mystery of the Church.

FIRST REFLECTION ON THE THEME
Living the Mystery of the Church

A. POINTS FOR MEDITATION

1. The world to come will be to the present world what the risen Christ is to Christ born of Mary; there will be continuity of being. The rupture of the end of the world will not be a break but a passage in which the omnipotence of God will be manifested.

2. It is man's part to guide the present world to the extreme limits of its possible becoming in view of glory, just as Christ, in view of his own resurrection, guided to adulthood the human being that he had received from Mary.

3. Christ as man was an element of the universe individualized through his relationships with the different environments in which his human being plunged its roots. In like manner, the Church recognizes in the universe the origin of its human substance and the environment from which its characteristic traits are elaborated.

4. The present world can pursue and achieve itself only by putting technology to work for it. Reflection on the meaning of technological effort is therefore indispensable to the Christian of today so that he may collaborate in the accomplishment of God's plan.

5. The provisional character of all results obtained through technical efforts can help the Christian detach himself from the dream of establishing definitive situations.

6. The will to progress that is essential to technological effort can make more authentic in the Christian the feeling of the precariousness of the present. The search for the best possible in the realm of material things has its equivalent in the duty to remain personally disengaged inside of a becoming.

7. There is a real convergence between the effort of technology to free man from the servitudes of sin and the saving power exercised over man by the risen Jesus Christ. To consecrate oneself to technological effort is therefore to colloborate in the plan of the redemption.

8. This convergence would cease if man gave to his technological efforts a finality that refused God's plan. To lend such a meaning to technological effort without any real foundation for so doing has been the most frequent tendency of Christians.

9. Rather than lend a "promethean" significance to technological efforts, it is better for the Christian to examine and judge himself, for it can easily happen that a religious man even in his purely religious activities will pursue ends that, in fact, are opposed to the plan of God.

10. One can embrace the earth to humiliate oneself in the sense of making oneself vile in one's own eyes. One can embrace the earth in the sense of recognizing and embracing the origin of one's being, which is matter. The gesture is symbolic and its value lies in its content. In the first case, we have, perhaps, an expression of the pride of the spirit, in the second, an act of authentic humility.

11. To embrace the earth today could be to embrace with fervor the technological realities that condition the material survival of humanity.

12. Perhaps the world expects of Christians that they teach it to give all its meaning to the embracing of the earth, that is technological effort, just as the first announcement of the risen Christ gave a meaning in those times to the pagan myths in which the love of the fruitful earth was expressed (Cybele, Anthea, etc.).

13. "Before they came together (Mary) was found to be with child of the Holy Spirit" (Mt. 1, 18). The universe was fruitful with the divine presence long before man erected the first sacred stone. It is not from the works of man that the world to come will be born. Yet this world to come can only be born from the availability of man to lend himself to the works of the Holy Spirit.

14. Just as Jesus Christ born of the Virgin Mary greeted Joseph with affection, calling him "father," so the Church, the mystical body of Christ born of the womb of humanity through the operation of the same Spirit must greet lovingly in the world and especially in the world of applied technology the "father," without whom she could not attain the fullness of her adult stature.

15. In two or three centuries from now when historians will speak of the Great Schism, they will not be speaking of the rupture that cut the Church in two, whether it separated East and West or opposed protestants and the faithful of Rome. This expression will be reserved for the most mysterious of schisms within the very constitution of the Church; this schism has dissolved the life of the Church as leukemia poisons the blood, that is, the separation between clergy and laity. This has reduced the laity to a state of minority under clerical tutelage and has caused the laity to disinterest themselves from the life of the Church that had become the sole business of clerics. It is significant that only the feminine world had continued to "form a mass" in the Church. It is not that woman is more religious than man, but only that woman has behind her a tradition of submissiveness that makes her less sensitive to a situation that man finds intolerable. But the woman of tomorrow will not be made of such stuff and it would be regrettable if we allowed ourselves to forget that she will not.

AND I DID NOT KNOW IT!

A. Permanent risk of falling back into practical ignorance of the "mystery of history": FAITH and structures.

The perspectives opened by reflection on the mystery of history are not very familiar to the majority of the faithful. How many of them live in a habitual awareness of this consecration of which humanity is the object?

Now, the first mission of the baptized is to live this consecration personally in such a manner that other men will also have the revelation of it through his person and give themselves to it (cf. 2 Cor. 4, 1, 2; 1 Pet. 3, 15ff.). As soon as this aspect is neglected or relegated to second place, the Christian becomes a man who has fallen back into practical ignorance of the mystery of history. This regression is the equivalent of making the revelation useless. It leads to a regression of faith in favor of structures.

FAITH, to express itself, needs external structures, gestures, objects, customs, places, forms of life, and action.

The more one contents oneself with a precarious FAITH the more do structures take on weight and importance. It can thus occur that by imposing their own laws over a length of time, structures that were born of FAITH make possible in the depths of collective or individual man a slow but certain ejection of that FAITH.

This draining away of FAITH can be detected in this, that the presence of God is no longer seen in the events of life. All relations with God are concentrated in the service of a reality that is deemed to be sacred, and according to circumstances one makes oneself the promoter or guardian, the herald or the defender of this reality.

Yesterday, one could see the faithful (clergy and laity) consecrating themselves above all to the erection of monuments and statues, to the propagation of devotions, and to the assistance of the prosperity of enterprises bearing religious labels. This was their passion and they lived only for it. Today, it is not expressed so much in material objects as in networks and zones of influence. The passion

146

then takes on forms of intolerance; one claims exclusive rights for the benefit of Catholic Action movements, for the group or the association in which one has been able to find, each one according to his own personality, a field for expansion.

It is legitimate for a Christian to be fond of some reality or another because it corresponds to a trait of his own temperament or nature. Even material objects must be admitted as means to reach the Lord who gave full consent to their utilization, as he has made of some of them the effective means of his presence in us. And the same can be said of the organizations in which the Church expresses its life. They have their value, and are an integral part of the ecclesial institution. But the moment that material objects or visible organizations are the object of excessive (and above all exclusive) attachment, the Christian falls back into practical ignorance of the mystery of history. He ceases to see God, the ascendancy inherited from his ancestors, and the spirit of the pagan religions lives again in him. Attached to objects, he becomes once more the adept of primitive religions by which man wanted to constrain the divinity and assign it to a residence (cf. Col. 2, 16-23). Attached to institutions he returns to the mentality of Israel according to the flesh aspiring to subject to the Lord, at the price of raids and massacres, a universe in which there had not yet been revealed to him the presence of God. In one case as in the other, by allowing oneself to be possessed by a cherished reality, one ceases to lend oneself to the action of the Holy Spirit, who alone makes the Church. Enslaved to structures one is condemned to a dulling of the FAITH.

B. A new "vision" makes us see God in everything but first of all, in the lives of men. "I knew it not," said Jacob. "Once more I was about to forget it," says the Christian as he ends a review of his life made in company with his brothers, noticing how easily one can escape the action of the Spirit by making God a thing, an object, or an institution with which one has fallen in love.

The review of life allows a Christian not to leave the mystery of history, which is the very mystery of the Church. Thanks to this review, he sees the living God, who, through his creative will and his will to communicate himself is personally engaged in the destiny of the universe. He has made the world of humans his home (Heb. 3, 6).

In this world of humans, the eye of the Christian discovers without difficulty on all levels and in all imaginable situations the perpetual presence of God, and this vision produces in him an immense respect for the majesty of God perceived in each man.

As Father, God is present to each man he creates at the very source of beginning of our being. As Son, God is present to each man. He remains the final inspiration of our being despite all the deficiencies we inherit from sin.

As Holy Spirit God is present to each man. He re-creates in us from that which we now are the new being who is promised incorruptibility (cf. 2 Cor. 1, 21-22).

"I am in the midst of you, I who am holy." When we realize this, we understand what it is to see the living God. We see the living God when we adore his presence and his action in all that is, but more particularly in human beings in whom he is at work accomplishing his eternal plan (cf. Jn. 5, 17). Far from feeling any need to make God a thing in some visible reality, we are able to act as if we saw the invisible (cf. Heb. 12, 27). We detect the Lord in situations from which he might have seemed to be the most absent, in our own sins, and even in situations from which we would spontaneously judge him to be the most absent, the sin of others, and the sin of the world.

We can understand here how un-Christian are the pessimistic judgments we sometimes make that condemn life and the world. We are willing to tell ourselves that these judgments come from our zeal for the glory of the Lord. In reality, they may well express only our more or less unconscious irritation at having been unable to impose on life, on the world, and on our times the image we ourselves had made of them and in which, of course, we had our places.

We can then apply to ourselves the words of St. Luke in his 19th chapter when he describes the disappointment of the inhabitants of Jericho when they saw Jesus lodging at the home of the ill-famed Zacchaeus. The text is significant because of the use the Church has made of it.

When it came to choosing a passage of the Gospel to express the mystery of the dedication, the Church chose neither the episode of the merchants driven from the Temple nor the passage relative to the life of the Lord in the family sanctuary of Nazareth, nor did she choose one of the texts that tell us of the intimate relations that made a home for Jesus from the house of Lazarus and his sisters. Mother and mistress of teaching in the name of the Spirit, the Church has chosen the story of the incident of Zacchaeus with the words of the Lord, "He also is a son of Abraham," followed by the commentary of the primitive Christian community, "the Son of man is come to seek and save that which was lost."

Of Zacchaeus and his house the so-called just men of Jericho could have said: "Surely the Lord was in this place and we knew it not."

Conclusions: Learn to hear the word of God that time is for us.
"We did not know it." Even today, two thousand years after the Word made flesh came into the world and the Holy Spirit was poured forth on men, God remains for many, even for Christians, the unknown God of whom St. Paul spoke to the Athenians (cf. Acts 22, 29). While in this God "we live and move and have our being," the incorrigible impulse of our weakness tends to make of him a thing in some idol, an object or a person, a rule or an institution, an edifice or an organization.

Scripture teaches us to see the living God; it makes us attentive to hear the mysterious word of God that is time. Of every event in our lives, as of the whole course of history, it teaches us to say in wonder with Jacob, "this is no less than a house of God and the gate of heaven . . . surely the Lord was there . . . and I knew it not!"

This understanding of time is not improvised. Man cannot even give it to himself; he can only dispose himself to receive it by asking it from God. A gift of God, it is given to the pure of heart, that is, as St. Francis expresses it, to those "who despise earthly things and always seek those of heaven and who never cease to adore and contemplate the Lord God living and true with a pure heart and mind" (*Admonitions* 16).

But this purity of heart and mind that allows the signs of the times to be perceived is measured by the silence that one will have had the courage to maintain in the presence of the events and happenings of life.

And more than to anyone else this silence is indispensable to the cleric who, full of the theoretical knowledge of the mystery of God, is the one man who needs the most to keep silent in the presence of the mystery of history. If he knows how to keep silent before the world and time, thus testifying of enough true love for the world and his own times, he will hear their voices. Beyond his theoretical knowledge of God he will then penetrate in depth into the true knowledge of the Lord in living the mystery of the Church.

SECOND REFLECTION ON THE THEME
Living the Mystery of the Church

A. Points for Meditation

1. The dream of leading the world is difficult to combine with effective collaboration in the plan of God (2 Cor. 6, 2; Is. 55, 8). Trying to make the Church triumph can result in dechristianizing the Church. The poor and the humble are then the first to discover themselves to be on the outside.

2. The dream of converting others, far from proceeding from FAITH, may only express the need to annex others to structures that are dear to us.

3. It is not unknown that believers, by their attitudes toward men they wish to convert, manifest behavior similar to a master race addressing inferior races.

4. By true FAITH, man breaks away from pessimistic judgments as well as from attitudes of conquest. FAITH makes man subject to all creatures. Indeed, true FAITH is for man the revelation of the universal presence of God. But this revelation is given to man only when he "converts himself to the Lord" (2 Cor. 3, 16), that is, when he effectively consents to allow the Lord to be in all truth the Lord in his life. This conversion to the Lord purifies the heart of man and allows him to see God.

5. When the Christian makes of God a thing in some reality that he cherishes (customs, religious traditions, organisms, etc.), this reality takes on the likeness of an idol and ends by forming a screen

between this Christian and the living God. One can then be emptied of FAITH all the while that one is working for religion.

B. PARTICULAR THEMES

Clergy and Laity

It can happen that Christians (above all in troubled times) show themselves to be avid for revelations (La Salette, Fatima). This is a bad sign. This taste for revelations testifies that one is overlooking the meaning of revelation. The veil has closed again before the eyes of the Christian. He no longer sees the living God.

Clerics

1. It can happen that clerics (both men and women) brought back to the true dimensions of their ministry, experience a feeling of frustration. "But then, what am *I* doing here?" The preoccupation of seeing to a proper respect for a hierarchic order in which they have their own place marked has perhaps altered in them the meaning of the salvation brought by Christ (cf. 1 Tim. 2, 4).

2. One frequently hears clerics repeat that "this era does not have FAITH." It would be better to say that this time cannot accommodate itself to expressions of FAITH with which earlier times were satisfied. Attitudes contrary to or opposed to FAITH are an invitation to reflect on the life of the Church. Often, these attitudes express an urgent demand for purification.

3. Marxist dialectic is in our time the formulation of thought that is the most opposed to FAITH. We can categorize it as error, or start from it to find a point of departure for reflection on the life of the Church and for a better consciousness of the realities of history.

It is a reminder that history is a mystery that is in the process of developement. It is a proof that a philosophy of essences is insufficient to explain all of reality. It is a restoration of the dialogue as the first instrument in the elaboration of an historic conscience. It is light thrown on the primacy of Christ by the abandonment of a juridical type of primacy (which is only a consequence of the former) to the benefit of an existential type of primacy (monogenesis of finality). The demanding requirements of purification that accompany this reflection will profit the whole Church and will be a step forward in the better knowledge of God as he has revealed himself to men. This is not giving in to an opinion of the moment, but is recognizing dialectical thought as an approach to total reality. History being dominated by the Person of the Word (the Logos), its development is necessarily dialectical. This development is accomplished by a confrontation of consciences expressing themselves in partial formulations. The confrontation results in a series of deadlocks whose issue can only be synthetic and successive reformulations. The last reformulation will be elaborated when the Person of the Word of God will have made all things subject in the Total Christ and accomplishes thus the unity of conscience of the living.

B. Texts for Reading and Prayer

a. Biblical Texts

One can reread different biblical stories, for example, in the Books of Samuel and Kings. Throughout these tales, one will seek to discern the action of God taking man just as he is and leading him toward his last end.

Jer. 29, 1-15. Reflect on events and in them "see" God.

Amos. 3, 3-9. It is God speaking in that which torments man.

Zeph. 3, 3-9. Purified through trials, Israel learns to recognize God present and acting within it.

Acts 10, 15.

Lk. 16, 19-27. The rich man has had his consolations on this earth. These consolations are the attachments that close one's eyes to the presence of God in others and in life.

Mt. 13, 3-44. Parables that underline the part played by time in the accomplishment of God's plan.

Parables of the Kingdom (cf. Mt. 12, 18—21, 25) and images that foreshadow the Church in the Old Testament (Eve, the Ark, the People, the Temple) furnish us with approaches. We can discern in them a common factor. There is always question of a dynamic reality that is in process of growth. Example, the Ark of Noah is not only a refuge, it is above all the germ of all repopulation (cf. Gen. 2; 8; Num. 11; 2. Sam. 7).

2 Cor. 5, 16-19; 6, 1. There is nothing to do but to lend oneself to a plan that is preparing a new creation.

b. Books

St. Francis, *Rule,* 1, chaps. 14 and 16; *Admonitions.*

c. Prayers

2. Sam. 22. David recognizes in what way God has been present to him.
Neh. 9, 5ff. Israel sees God present in all of its history.
Pss. 42; 43; 63. Ardent desire to "see" God.
Ps. 73. Only the man with a pure heart keeps his view clear.

Final Theme

1 Tim. 3, 15.

PART THREE: CONCLUSIONS

The third word that God addresses to man is the times in which man lives. Through attentive listening to his own times, the person completely situates himself in the truth of his own condition. He accepts himself as being within a becoming, and of this becoming each man represents only a moment.

It is not easy for man to accept this dependence in regard to his times. It is even less easy to accept dependence in regard to a time whose successive moments are growing more and more different.

Meditation on Scripture facilitates this acceptance. Throughout the vicissitudes of the history of Israel, Scripture reveals to man the meaning of the evolutions that he is called upon to live in the course of the ages.

As much on a personal as on a collective level, man can live the successive evolutions only by involving himself in them. It is a matter of going forward in FAITH in a God of whom one knows—he has proven it—that he is LOVE.

Going forward in FAITH supposes that one does not allow himself to be stopped by any of the visible realities, or images, with which one may have become infatuated. They must all be passed by in a gesture of poverty that purifies HOPE.

This purification makes it possible for man to understand life and the world. The eyes of man open themselves to the mystery of history. He experiences REVELATION because God is seen in everything and everything is seen as being filled with God.

PART FOUR
Living the Mystery of Easter

I

Communion with the Father

"Let nothing please and delight us except our Creator"

St. Francis. *First Rule,* 23

"WHATEVER OVERCOMES A MAN TO THAT HE IS ENSLAVED" (2 Pet. 2, 19).

A. In man, the summit of the universe, the entire universe is called upon to make the PASSAGE that returns the world to God.

Taken from nothingness by the Word of God (cf. Heb. 11, 3), the universe is developing itself since its origin to RETURN to GOD.

The universe accomplishes this RETURN to GOD through successive stages. It passes from the so-called inferior stages to the superior stages. It passes thus from energy to atom, from atom to molecule, then from molecule to microorganism and from microorganism to vegetable life, from vegetable life to sensitive life that is conditional and from conditional life to freedom. At each of these stages, what is created passes on to a state of development greater than its preceding state. The state of freedom represents the most perfect state in the natural order.

The universe attains this state of freedom in the human being. In a way, the world of men represents the supreme expression of the level that the universe attained through the simple expansion of the dynamism received from the creative word (cf. Heb. 1, 3). When the human being appeared in the world, the universe crossed the frontiers of divinity through image and resemblance (cf. Gen. 1, 26). That which came forth from dust revealed itself to be capable of surpassing its own determinations as dust.

157

But this state of freedom is itself only a stage. For the creature to RETURN to God, an ultimate PASSAGE must be made from the state of freedom to the state of COMMUNION.

God is COMMUNION (cf. Jn. 1, 4), and to RETURN to God is to enter the current of exchanges that is the LIFE of the three Persons, Father, Son and Holy Spirit in the unique nature of God.

This ultimate PASSAGE, man, the summit and the term of all the effort of the universe, could not accomplish by himself. But it was in the plan of God to give man this power as a free gift.

At the end of the necessary preparations (the fullness of time) God proposed to make man a participant in his own divine nature by becoming a man himself (cf. 2 Pet. 1, 4). The Word of God was made flesh by espousing in man the condition of flesh. In God, the Son made man, every man by grace will become a son of God (cf. Jn. 1, 12; 1 Jn. 3, 1). In thus introducing the flesh into the bosom of God, the creative Word will achieve its work through the RETURN of the world to God (cf. Jas. 1, 18).

B. The PASSAGE has been made impossible for man by sin, which alters in him the state of freedom. This ultimate PASSAGE, impossible for the forces of nature, man, the summit and head of nature, has tried to accomplish on his own. He has thought that he could give to himself the-going-beyond-himself to which God called him freely.

"You will be like God" (Gen. 3, 5).

Man has paid dearly for this impossible venture; he emerged crippled. The original downfall not only broke the relations of friendship between man and God that God had graciously established with him in prevision of Christ but also altered in man the fragile balance that had been slowly elaborated during thousands of years of uninterrupted preparations and successive passages. Man was wounded in his aptitude to pass beyond the determinisms of existence, and was wounded in his capacity to be free.

Imagine a rocket in flight. At a certain point in its ascent, it will be free of gravitational pull and will pursue its course solely through the laws of universal attraction and will continue without being subject to wear or attrition. A false maneuver could, however, modify its course and prevent its becoming free of the earth's gravitational pull. It would then be unable to break away, and would fall and disintegrate. So it is with the universe.

The impulse given by God to his work led creation to a state of freedom and through the simple action of grace, which is an all powerful attraction, man surpassed his own natural momentum to enter and participate in incorruptible life.

But man has aspired to impose his own will on nature and the course of events. The impulse of the universe no longer carries him to the threshold of the ultimate passage. He is condemned to a fall that is disintegration and death for him. Through the fault of man, the universe does not RETURN to God.

It is a fact that in fallen man the work of creation has, in a way, been made less than it should be. It has descended lower than the human level because man, its summit, has been found finally to be inferior to that which the universe, upheld by the all powerful Word, had made him to be. The wound affects all creation (cf. Rom. 8, 19f.). It affects man in the basic elements of his being, the biological equilibrium of his cells. This balance is henceforth condemned to wear and attrition and finally to disintegration and death. The sum total of all of these imbalances affects man in that which precisely makes him a man—his condition of freedom. Injured in his aptitude to give himself to others, how can he ready himself to make the PASSAGE to the state of COMMUNION?

C. By assuming our condition of slavery and death Christ makes the PASSAGE possible again. God, however, did not renounce his plan to give his creation its full achievement by the introduction of man into his own life. But since man had reduced himself to a state below that of his original condition, it became necessary for God to come and seek man in the condition of diminished freedom to which he had been brought through his own pride.

To this end the Word of God in becoming flesh espoused not only man's nature but also the condition which man had made for himself through sin. Christ is born "under the law" (Gal. 4, 4).

Of course the flesh that the Word of God assumed in the womb of the Virgin was a flesh already restored to its original purity. In the human being of Christ as in the being of his immaculate Mother, everything was harmony, a condition of freedom, and aptitude to enter into COMMUNION. This flesh of Christ was even here below fully one with the Father in the Person of the Word (cf. Jn. 14, 2). In this flesh, the PASSAGE to the Father encountered neither limitation nor obstacle (cf. Mt. 17, 2).

But did not Christ as Son of man owe it to himself to live his PASSAGE to the Father in complete solidarity with his brothers (cf. Heb. 2, 12. 15)? It was necessary (cf. Lk. 24, 26). This perspective was for him a source of anguish (cf. Lk. 12, 50), but he desired, nonetheless, with a great desire to make this PASSAGE with us (cf. Lk. 22, 15), that is, to take upon himself all the conditions in which the PASSAGE would be accomplished for each man (cf. Heb. 2, 9).

Christ in the fullness of his liberty allows himself to die (cf. Jn. 10, 17). Just like any other son of man, the Son of God becomes a corpse that is buried in the ground. Thus does he participate in the falling back that death is for every man.

Now beyond this falling back, Christ returned from the tomb. He passed to his Father with the totality of his human being—spirit and matter. By this resurrection, he guarantees to men that even when they are laid beneath the earth, they also shall rise and the totality of their being, matter and spirit, will make the passage to COMMUNION with the Father.

"Right hand" of the Father, Christ came to take man by the hand at the lowest point of the condition that fallen man had been able to make for himself—the tomb (cf. Ps. 118, 16f.).

Since Christ has accomplished the PASSAGE in complete solidarity with men, the life of men has once again found its full significance; it has become the preparation for a state that is to come.

Inheritor of the millions of years that have made it possible, the life of men has meaning only because it prepares a condition to come that will at once surpass and fulfill all the aspirations that express themselves in it. In the human being are fulfilled all the surpassing that occurs in animal life in regard to vegetable life, and in vegetable life as regards so-called inert matter. The human being who recapitulates all these knows that in Christ, he is promised a beyond that will at one and the same time surpass and fulfill all his deepest expectations, because in this beyond will be recapitulated all the successive stages that have prepared it.

This is the true greatness of the human condition, the ultimate expression that the created universe can give of itself and the preparation of a beyond that far surpasses the universe. But this greatness must not make man forget that the going beyond to be accomplished requires of him that he start from his real condition, a state of degradation caused by sin, a state of diminished freedom.

Conclusions: The fundamental task of the Christian is to restore the original state of freedom by referring himself to Christ. "By the uncreated Word of God, man has come into being. By withdrawing himself from the Word of God, the deep inspiration of his being, man has fallen into degradation. By referring himself to the Word of God made flesh, man recovers his integrity."

Summing up in these lines his total vision of the world, St. Bonaventure invites man to expect his full restoration only in reference to Christ. The man who wills to be submissive to Christ will, first of all, recognize that he is in a fallen state of diminished freedom, and he will take as his first and essential task the restoration in and around himself of the original state of freedom. To do this, he will follow Christ and place all his own freedom in his consent to suffer, to die, to become a corpse, that is to be buried, and he will do this in the same measure that suffering and death are required of him to break the determinations in which sin imprisons him.

But it must be understood that to refer oneself thus to Christ is not possible for the sole forces of man; it is a gift of God, the result of an attraction exercised on our being by God (cf. Jn. 6, 44). This is why if man wishes to be free once more, he must aspire with all his soul to be drawn to the Father. This attraction, far from diminishing or altering the freedom we already enjoy, can only strengthen and confirm in us whatever is authentic in this freedom, for the attraction exercised by God on our being is necessarily in profound accord with the being we receive from him.

St. Francis of Assisi had indeed experienced this harmony between the attraction exercised on us by God and the deep reality of our human nature: "let nothing please and delight us except our Creator and Redeemer" (*First Rule*, 23).

Through the conjunction between our own vital dynamisms and the attraction exercised on us by God the Father, we can hope individually as well as collectively that we may be restored to a state of freedom that is real enough to make possible for us once again the PASSAGE to COMMUNION with the Father.

FIRST REFLECTION ON THE THEME
Communion with the Father

A. POINTS FOR MEDITATION

1. Man is not born free. He owes it to himself to become free.

2. Man can be free only to the degree that he becomes free. To enslave others to free oneself is to reduce oneself to slavery. One is the slave to the need to have slaves and to the necessity of keeping these slaves in slavery.

3. In past centuries, man could become free more easily because he could in a way live in ignorance of the dimensions of the human world. Today, it is more difficult for man to have access to freedom because the problems of the ends of the earth are henceforth a part of the problem of his own freedom.

4. The freedom to which the man of today can have access is a truer, deeper, and more total freedom than that enjoyed by the man who came before him, in the sense that it is better informed of its own determinations and limits.

5. Materialism always enslaves man, whether it states in what it is about (philosophical materialism) or goes on to do so without any statements (practical materialism).

6. If the conditions in which I am able to enjoy life are made possible for me through conditions in which others are crushed, I am a slave to the need to have these others as slaves. This is practical materialism.

7. Every refusal to allow another to have access to true freedom

is a contribution to the maintenance of the situation that results from sin.

8. The systems that preach the maintenance of privileged situations (whether of individuals, social classes or continents) are through this maintenance of systems of slavery offering a practical refusal to the salvation Christ brought to men.

9. The stirrings of sensuality in the human being are a reawakening (due to sin) of states that are anterior to the human state. It is less a matter of eliminating these stirrings through discipline than of reintegrating the energies that they disperse by giving to them once more the meaning that they were intended to have in a condition of freedom. This state of freedom was a preparation of the human being with the aim of having him love with the love with which God loves. To apply oneself to love with this love contributes to the restoration of the equilibrium of the senses in man. The restoration of balance of the senses favors the progress of true love in him. All forms of chastity (religious, clerical, conjugal, adolescent, and adult) will be a problem to those who question themselves on these matters without having this perspective before their mind.

"LIVE AS FREE MEN!" (1 Pet. 2, 16).

A. To become free once more demands renouncing the self-made images we have of ourselves.

Reflection on the reality of our human condition tells us that freedom is not a good that man holds at the beginning of his journey; it is the fruit of a restoration that is gradually acomplished in us.

We become free by lending ourselves day after day to the liberations that God, through the interplay of existence, makes possible for us. These successive liberations break one after another the chains that were binding freedom in us.

Now all of these chains can be reduced finally to an image that each one of us gloats upon inside of himself.

To be preoccupied with an idea of self enslaves man, individually as well as in a group. He then lives only to justify, to defend and if necessary, to impose on others, the traits of this image whose slave he has become. All the dynamism of the person (or of a group of persons) consumes itself in subjecting everything—self, others, the time in which one lives—to this image. One ends by annexing all reality, even if this makes it necessary to place it on the procustean bed this image has set up.

The first stage of our liberation will therefore consist in identifying the characteristics of this image of which sin has made us the slaves. Only then will we be able to break ourselves away from the determinations of the state of degradation and be ready for the advance into our true becoming—the life of God.

There, too, it will become necessary to go from inferior to superior states. The advance will be accomplished by successive passages.

There must be, first of all, an effort to detach oneself from past influences such as infantile, childish, and adolescent mentality, and also from the mentalities of the different stages of what has been called the adult age. But we must also be aware of the far more enslaving force of the simultaneous mentalities formed in us through our environment, professional interests, social class, race, times, and location. Nor must we forget to consider the elements formed in us by temperament, the education we have received, and the influences we have encountered.

The Lord is constantly warning Israel in the scriptures against the danger that is a "hardening of heart" (cf. Ps. 95, 8). The baptized person must watch and guard against letting himself be hardened or structured by anything. We must therefore know the forces that lead us from the inside, but we must also be aware of the currents that govern us from outside, whether we allow ourselves to be captured blindly or whether we resist them.

Each trait of the image of ourselves that we can identify may become for us a cause of anguish when we discover its lack of authenticity. It is a new birth, the entry into a mode of being to which we are not accustomed and that we have reason to fear. But at each stage, this new birth makes true freedom grow in us, that freedom given by the truth. Torn from the illusion that would have been the success of a false image of ourselves, we are freed from the lie that has imprisoned man in death.

This liberation is not the work of our own forces; it is Christ who operates it in us through the strength of his life.

This power has, in a certain way, entered into us by the sacrament of baptism, but it remains for us, so that this power of life may be able to act in us, to live effectively the mystery in which we have been plunged by this sacrament.

To live the mystery of our baptism is to accept without rejecting them all the events of existence that impinge on us; each in its own way is some kind of death or burial. These deaths can be numerous and the burials endure for a long time. But we must tell ourselves that man is in need of time and many fresh starts before, like a "grain of wheat" (cf. Jn. 12, 24), he descends deeply enough into his own soil to be able to take root there in truth. There only will he be born to true freedom in the truth of his earthly condition, in the image of Christ rising to glory from his burial in the tomb (cf. 1 Cor. 15, 39-57; Col. 2, 12; 3, 1-12). Above all, to live this mystery is to bury *ourselves* in the *truest* way in our own *personal* condition of earth. For the most difficult thing is not to accept burial, to refuse to see and then to accept in what this burial must consist.

There is a danger here especially if one is impressed with the findings of psychology. It could happen that one markedly avoids the insight that others around him (children included) give him into himself. This might continue for a lifetime. The same refusal to face oneself might also be present when confronted with the director or psychologist one claims to consult.

Thus we see individuals who have recourse to "burials" that are the means for them to avoid any step forward into the mystery of the death and burial of the Lord. They withdraw from all contacts into practical isolation, the silence of a cloister, a schedule of hyperactivity, or the refusal of any activity, at all. Far from preparing any liberation of our being, these burials are the construction of enclosures where that which is the least free in man will be able to flourish imprudently under sacred labels.

It does not come spontaneously to man, nor even easily, to hold himself open to the truth (cf. Gal. 6, 13; Jn. 7, 32).

B. We can rid ourselves of pres- Christian spiritual writers have **tige, especially if it is sacred,** given to the image of self to **only if we realize that this life** which every human being can be- **is a preparation.** come a slave the traditional name of "self-importance."

The danger of this self-importance grows all the greater when the Christian, on account of his responsibilities, makes the image he has fabricated of himself into something sacred.

In the name of what he represents or incarnates, a man through his spontaneous behavior can come to glory in those things that lessen him as a man. Such are the impediments that come from temperament (whether atavistic or hereditary), or from habits that have been contracted, from badly directed tendencies, from insufficiently controlled impulses, and from trials and humiliations that have not yet been adequately dealt with.

If the Christian makes of that which makes him less of a man a sort of good to be jealously retained, he is imprisoning himself in a new slavery, taking himself away from the PREPARATION and making it very difficult for himself, despite the grace of his baptism, to make the PASSAGE with Christ. We know the meaning of the step taken by the Lord Jesus Christ to be found as a man, he did not count equality with God as a thing to be grasped but emptied himself. Self-importance is never more dangerous than when it uses the glory of God as an argument to defend itself (cf. Ph. 2, 6).

In each Christian are repeated the struggles and tensions that were lived in Egypt during the first pasch. Pharaoh, who does not want to hear of freedom for the People of God, is opposed by Moses who has come to claim this freedom in the name of God (cf. Exod. 6, 7.8).

Each Christian carries Moses in himself, the Holy Spirit given from above who calls to freedom and leads to life. But each Christian also carries within himself Pharaoh, the spirit of self, the depravation from below that enslaves and leads to death.

Now this spirit of self in man is capable of operating wonders and prodigies (including prodigies of virtue) so as to mislead the calls of the Holy Spirit; thus the magicians of Pharaoh played a trick on Moses as they rivaled him in their ability to perform miracles.

The cult of physical strength or of physical beauty, the cult of one's own moral or spiritual qualities, the vanity of youthful successes or status, and influential relationships in the adult or the aging—it matters little, for the moment that one is satisfied with what one is or what one possesses one ceases to live the preparation, one becomes congealed and is paralyzed. Then one devotes oneself to polishing oneself in the condition in which one happens to be, the determinisms of the law of gravity are then complicated and weighted down with all the seductive prestige put to work by self-importance and man thus becomes capable of loving his chains enough to take glory in them.

Now we must tear ourselves away from all enslavements. And enslavements that are very real are not always felt to be enslavements. They are felt less as they are the more glamorous (cf. Heb. 11, 24.28).

We must live our existence (both individual and collective) as the celebration of a pasch. To celebrate this pasch does not consist in repeating, "alleluia, alleluia," with joyous optimism. We will have understood very little about the mystery of the pasch if we see in it the assurance of a final victory of the type who laughs last, and best.

The understanding of the pasch begins to grow in us with meditation on the chapters of Exodus, when we become conscious that our personal as well as our collective being is weighed down beneath heavy chains.

The understanding of the pasch becomes perfect in us through meditation on the preparation lived in the person of Christ, the Word on the cross.

We gather from these two sacred texts the understanding of the mystery of our own existence. We learn from Exodus that every step by which we safeguard or restore in or around ourselves true freedom is a contribution to the preparation of our own passage and of the passage of the universe to its final achievement. We learn from the crucified Word that on account of sin, every step by which freedom is safeguarded or restored is necessarily painful.

But this painful preparation lived by Christ and the glory that came to him through the passage to his Father become for us for all time the true reasons to consent to suffer enough so that there may be restored in us and as much as possible around us as complete a condition as possible of true freedom (cf. 1 Cor. 15, 30f.).

C. This "preparation" is accomplished in us if in the lives we are leading we learn to love. The saints are those men who have suffered enough to be able to become once more truly free themselves and to make possible for the men that surround them the conditions of true freedom.

Pious imagery likes to represent the saints in ecstasy in an intimate communion with God or else afflicting some cruel mortification upon themselves.

The predominance of these two modes of representation is a sign of a state of mind that is frequently encountered. For the mass of the faithful, entry into communion with God can be obtained only at the cost of behavior that is extraordinary.

An objective attention to the lives of the saints should be sufficient to convince us of the contrary.

Of course, all the saints had to suffer, but suffering is actually the lot of all men. And the suffering that enables the saints to enter into communion with God is not that which they inflicted upon themselves; it is the suffering that they knew how to welcome and to bear in their own lives because they loved.

To love is, in the last resort, to need others. This "need of others" is not to be reduced to the avowal that others are indispensable to us for a home, for food and clothing, for electricity at the touch of a switch, for our daily newspaper and for gasoline along our highways. Such needs remain in the simple physical domain or, at most, the physiological one. The true need for others is that which is felt as an imperative in the depths of one's being, in that which his being possesses that makes it most truly human. We feel it deeply only after having vitally experienced that we are made by others as much as for others, and that others are necessary for the achievement of our person and that we cannot even contemplate existing without them.

The authentic need for others is felt by man only from the day when in some way there has arisen from the depths of his heart to his lips the avowal that lovers make to one another, "I cannot live without you."

This experience is felt individually by the awareness experienced by a youth of what friendship brings to him, by the realization made by a man or a woman of what his or her partner gives to him or to her, or of what their children mean to them. It is the awareness experienced by each one of us of what his community, his teammates, his natural surroundings mean to him. This awareness is also collective; no community can become completely human unless in and with other communities.

When this realization has finally led a man or a group of men to prefer suffering, and even should the occasion arise, death, to the greater detriment from which others must be preserved this man or this group of men have learned what it is to love.

This is the whole story of the saints. The saints, because they loved, knew how to suffer enough and because they suffered enough, they became free enough to be able to love more, and loving more, they were then made capable of suffering more. Thus, from liberation to liberation, they led their lives in preparation for the passage through which access is gained to communion with the Father, carrying like a wound in themselves the "need for others."

The progress in communion with God is never the reward or the fruit of a flight from others. The saints have known the Lord (communion with the Father) because they knew how to recognize him in others, that is in communion with their brothers (cf. Mt. 25, 40). Their example recalls that it is impossible for man to enter into the knowledge of God otherwise than through the knowledge of man. This impossibility is radical. A human being who in all his life would have never encountered another man could never know God. Except for a true miracle, this human being would not be in possession of the psychological instruments indispensable for entry into the knowledge of God. How could he enter into communion with the God he does not see if he has never had the occasion to enter into relations with the image that is visible? (Cf. 1 Jn. 4, 20.)

"Thou hast seen thy brother; thou hast seen thy God," said the Fathers of the Church to the Christians of the first centuries. And St. John, after a half century of reflection on the unique experience of his intimacy with Christ sums up his experience in these words: "He who loves is born of God and knows God. He who does not love does not know God" (1 Jn. 4, 7-8).

Conclusions: Prepare the PAS-SAGE to communion with the Father by assuming responsibility for the reality of existence.

Thus, man has access to the total accomplishment of his destiny in becoming free again, but he restores in himself the condition of freedom only in the measure of his own loving insertion into the normal network of his interhuman relations. The community of men is the bosom outside of which no one can prepare the passage to communion with the Father.

This loving insertion consists in assuming with loyalty and fidelity to the reality of this world our own person, environment, and times. There can be no question of moulding the world or ourselves according to an image of our own choices. The question is simply to assume without trying in any way to avoid them the real situations that are given to us by our existence in this world. Through this attitude, man becomes capable of suffering because he loves and because he has known how to suffer, he is made capable of loving more.

"Our Lord Jesus Christ," writes Francis of Assisi, "called his betrayer friend . . . therefore all those who unjustly inflict on us tribulations and anguish, shame and injuries, sorrows and torments, martyrdom and death are our friends whom we ought to love much because we gain eternal life by that which they make us suffer" (*First Rule*. Ch. 22).

To expect from life here below the possibility of a going beyond into eternal life allows a man to detach himself from a false image of himself. Valued according to what he is willing to endure, man hears himself told what a weight of real freedom has been restored to him. He can then know if the preparation has begun in him that will one day make it possible for him to pass on to the state of perfect communion with the Father.

SECOND REFLECTION ON THE THEME
Communion with the Father

A. POINTS FOR MEDITATION

1. The PREPARATION of *the world to come,* which will be the full and perfect COMMUNION with the Father is not made by the pursuit of dreams, even if these dreams are spiritual ones. This preparation is accomplished in the reality of existence.

2. In order to accomplish his dreams man needs only his intelligence and his will. He can even do with less, culture, influence, and on the lower level, with less force, cunning or money.

On the contrary, in order to assume human situations in their reality and to allow himself to be moulded through them, man must face the truth about himself. All he has is his capacity to suffer and if necessary, to die for those to whom he is indebted. Here, each man is weighed on a just scale as was Christ when he was suspended and weighed on the scales of the cross (cf. the hymn *Vexilla Regis*).

3. The worst and most dangerous enslavements are those in which a man encloses himself in the name of fidelity within an image of himself (as a Christian) or within an image of the Church as a society in which one possesses some title.

4. The total accomplishment of a being is determined by his

discovery that others are indispensable to the complete achievement of himself. This discovery, by causing man to be born to love, makes him capable of suffering enough to be able to empty himself of the leaven of selfishness and to become free once more.

5. One can have been free and after having been free become enslaved once more.

6. One can with eyes wide open not even *see* others (cf. Lk. 17, 19.27). He who ignores or classifies others cannot see them anymore. He cannot be in communion with the Father.

B. Particular Themes

Reflections for Priests

1. For the Church in the midst of humanity to make possible and obtain the preparation that will enable this humanity to make the PASSAGE to the Father, it is essential that churchmen do not entertain unwarranted ideas of themselves, but remain at the service of human reality. This availability to serve will be expressed on the part of clerics by the wish to be buried, as it were (cf. Col. 3, 3).

2. Because they are men (that is of the male sex), those who hold in their hands the responsibilities in the Church do not always know well enough the meaning of the feminine vocation of the Church. She is a handmaid following him who wished to be a servant. Like the woman who transforms her condition as wife into that of "boss," churchmen too preoccupied with the image of a Church that was to rule, have often given her a hard and domineering face. Codes and "property rights," manuals of morality, and zones of influence were sometimes deep wrinkles on a face in which humanity was no longer seeing Christ, but a power with which other secular powers had to reckon.

3. Because the Church is a visible institution, it is obliged to organize its life visibly. But in this organization, it can occur that clergymen are led by an image of themselves. They then enclose the Church in the defense of organisms and institutions. The energies of the Church are then wasted. This has occurred each time the Church has presented to men a face that is other than the femi-

nine face which the world of men needs so as not to become inhuman. The face of a poor and humble Church should be a presence, not a power, an inspiration, not a government.

4. When the cleric tries to make the Church totally masculine as he makes her an organizer, he is often expressing a dynamism that has not integrated the life of chastity. The chastity of the cleric and that of the religious have meaning only in view of the Kingdom. If chastity is not the expression of a greater love of Christ, the cleric will necessarily be brought to express in works, organizations, buildings, various forms of prestige, dynamisms that must be expressed. The worst faults against chastity are not necessarily the faults of the flesh.

C. TEXTS FOR READING AND PRAYER

a. Biblical Texts

First of all we will turn to the story of the first pasch, that in which God had foreshadowed the image of the real pasch made possible for every man by the passion, death, and resurrection of Jesus.

Exod. 6. Moses is the image of the Spirit of God who in our baptized hearts urges us to take our departure toward freedom.

Exod. 7; 8. To the events that must convince us, Pharaoh (the spirit of self) shows himself capable, like a real magician, of opposing, if necessary, accomplishments that are called miraculous.

Exod. 9; 12. Until that day when the Lord finally overcomes our resistances by striking a decisive blow through the trials of existence. . . .

Exod. 12; 15. Our true nature tearing itself away from the satisfactions of slavery. . . .

Exod. 16, 17.40. Enter the wilderness under the leadership of the Lord.

Exod. 23; Num. 9; 10. The community of all the People of God that forms the Church . . .

1 Cor. 15, 20-57. The beyond that is guaranteed to us in Christ.

2 Cor. 5, 1-10. Aspirations toward true liberation (cf. Rom. 8, 18-26).

Gal. 5, 1; Col. 3, 1-18. Expressions that express the freedom of the Christian.

1 Jn. 1, 3.4. The revelation made to us.

b. Books

Thomas of Celano, *Vita Prima.* Part I. chaps. 21-28.
St. Francis *Third Letters;* Rule II, chap. 6.

c. Prayers

    Pss. 105; 106; 107. These psalms, by relating the episodes through which God saved his People, allow us to imagine through what perils and risks of slavery we need to be led by God toward our final passage.

    Ps. 139. Homage rendered to God who possesses our being.

    We can return here with profit to the three stages of the First Step.

Final Theme

    1 Cor. 10, 11.

II
Submitting Ourselves to the Spirit

> "Love others as they are without desiring for thy
> sole advantage that they be better Christians."
>
> St. Francis, *Letter 3*

"ALL WERE MADE TO DRINK OF ONE SPIRIT"
(1 Cor. 12, 13).

A. To love by associating man with God's ACTION makes him enter into communion with God. The "need for others," when it is painfully lived, restores man to the state of original freedom. Relations with others are for him a preparation for entering into COMMUNION with the Father.

To be in COMMUNION with the Father is to share the life of the Father, the life of God.

The mystery of this life of God has been revealed to us. We know that in it, three Persons are indispensable. None of them can think or will independently of the other two. "God is LOVE" (1 Jn. 4, 8). This expression of St. John is the culmination of all revelation. It means that in God, all life is summed up and consumed in relationships that are the necessary ACTION of a unique nature expressing itself in three different Persons. This is God's way of life.

Made in his nature, in the image of God, man is called by grace to live the life of God. The fruit of a created universe, he will live a life that surpasses creation. It is not astonishing that man must in some way become an apprentice in the divine way of life.

This apprenticeship in divine ways man accomplishes in the action of interhuman relations. In the midst of these relations, the

175

need for others arouses in him as the expression of his innermost being the opening to relationships, that is, love. By opening himself to these, man is initiated into living the life of God. There is in this situation lived by each man a "wonder" of the care of God.

Wishing to make himself known to man, God does not give man a theory on his nature. Neither does he give him a practical demonstration of his power. But as a father makes himself known to his children by associating them with his own activities, God makes himself known to man by making him participate in his own DIVINE ACTION. The fundamental and necessary DIVINE ACTION is to love. To man it will therefore be given to love with the love with which God loves. Thus, man will come to know God in the sharing of God's life.

We know really well only those with whom we came into the world physically (brothers and sisters) and above all, psychologically (parents and children, husband and wife together). To make himself known to us, God has thought of having us come into being with him by making us participants in his own activity. Loving, which is the gift of self to others, associates us with the ACTION itself of God. We enter into the true knowledge of God, the knowledge that is COMMUNION with God.

The promise constantly repeated throughout Scripture, "Thou shalt know the Lord," is accomplished when for a man to live is to love. Of course, there can only be question of loving with the love with which God loves.

B. Our being can arrive at loving truly only by placing itself under the direction of the Holy Spirit. Let us first establish as a principle that every exercise of the ACTION by which a human being loves necessarily associates him with the ACTION of God who is love. Of course, it is necessary that this human ACTION express an authentic love.

Now, human ACTION implies a mobilization of the dynamism of our being in a given direction. ACTION arouses in us the fundamental drives of our being. These drives are necessarily accompanied by a narrowing of the field of vision of our conscience. A man caught up in ACTION sees less clearly what is leading him on. This man may think that he loves because he wears himself out by giving himself when he is simply the slave of his temperament, his habits, perhaps even of some preconceived notion.

This is because of the implacable thirst for immediate success (the image of self) that pursues man even in the ACTION wherein he gives himself. This ACTION must be counterbalanced by an ENDURANCE welcomed as an indispensable element of the self-success which is to be accomplished. Slow rate of growth, weariness of fresh starts in the face of obstacles, acceptance of failure that is indispensable to the purification of the pursued objective—all these are necessary elements in the realization of an authentic love.

Now it can occur that instead of welcoming this indispensable endurance, we refuse it. The obstacle stirs in us the impetuosity of ACTION. Seized and possessed by his plans, his ideas and his views while he works for those he thinks he loves (God as well as "others") man begins to employ means, proceedings and influences that are no longer in the order of an ACTION that God can assume and place to the account of his own divine ACTION.

The temptation to excess therefore threatens man even in a move that should associate him with God's ACTION itself. One can thus make oneself incapable of loving truly with the love with which God loves through the excess with which he regards his self-giving or altruism.

True love is, first of all, "feeling for the other." This feeling for the other (of which modesty is a natural expression) does not allow us to impose ourselves upon him. Nor can we impose ourselves on his weakness, his ignorance, his suffering, or his poverty. Whoever loves truly knows how to bring and to offer to the other only what the other has already desired to receive. God is the perfect image of this respect for the other; he does not impose himself on man. He knows how to wait for man to desire him (cf. Mt. 5, 45). This respect for the other does not exist when one goes to him with the superiority of one who gives, who protects, or who saves.

To give, to protect, and to save often lead man (individually and collectively) to treat the other as a simple outlet for a domestic economy that is short of markets in which to expand. The other is not loved; he does not even exist anymore. He has been made into an object. Above all there is no respect for the other when one goes to him with the self-assurance of one who seems to know everything.

He who knows might have his eyes wide open, but he will not see the other. Because one knows, one notifies another of the truth. He classifies and condemns. One no longer sees the other but simply his intelligence to be possessed. To love others we must be profoundly convinced that no one possesses the truth but that all must allow themselves to be taken and possessed by it, above all, those who have received it from Christ and from the irreplaceable light of revelation. It is therefore very important for believers, especially if they are priests, to impose on themselves an absolute respect for others, for religious intentions and so-called supernatural plans can simply make possible situations in which man is even further deluded about the quality of the love with which he thinks he loves.

The refusal of difficulties in the order of ENDURANCE is characteristic of all situations in which the human being (individually or collectively) will believe that he loves when in reality he is only willing his own expansion. It is not unlikely to find that one has arrived at not loving at all while one "kills" oneself for persons who are supposed to be cherished (God and others). But this human ACTION that God in assuming would have transmuted into the gold of CHARITY will be nothing but dust and straw (cf. 1 Cor. 3, 10-18). The refusal or the overlooking of the difficulties and limits of ENDURANCE results in making even a generous ACTION something that is no longer able to be assumed within the ACTION of God.

We now have some idea of the character of human action that would be associated with the action of God, who is love. This action cannot be a simple collection of tropisms, the surge of instinct. Nor can it be merely the expansive tendency of someone who is looking for ways to express this. Love must express one's entire being. It is an exchange; it endures, and is an action. It is the gift of self. But just as important, it is acceptance of other persons and of everything that we will suffer for them and because of them.

Thus love far surpasses the forces of man weighed down by sin. But the seed of this love has been sown in the most intimate place in man's heart by the Holy Spirit (cf. Rom. 5, 5). Received at baptism, it grows in to the degree that we acquiesce to the impulses of the life of which he introduces the mysterious power into us (cf. Eph. 4, 30). To submit oneself to the Holy Spirit is to learn to love.

C. The Holy Spirit helps us to   Life teaches man that even on
love with the love with which   occasions when he thought most
God loves.   sincerely that he loved another, it
may have happened that he only
loved an image of himself. In giving over his body to fire (cf. 1 Cor.
13, 3), a Christian can remain outside of God's love and therefore
outside of communion with God.

But life is also the school in which man learns to love, the human
condition (nature) and divine inspiration (grace) are joined there to
initiate man into loving with an authentic love.

This interplay of nature and grace tend to free man of the illusion that supreme wisdom would consist in needing no one at all.

Whether through the will to love only God, from ambition to
live for some great cause, or by preoccupation not to create problems for oneself, some Christians make it their rule at times to restrain in themselves any impulse of affection.

Whether through a sudden awakening of their repressed nature
or, if late in life by some situation that places them at the mercy of
anothers care, they will be saved by accepting the need for others.

This motion, even if it is only a passive gesture of their last hour,
will finally allow the flowering and even the full blooming within
them of the aptitude to love. They will cease to offer to God only a
crippled human nature; the Holy Spirit will finally gain hold of them
and taking charge of their conduct (cf. Rom. 8, 14) will initiate
them into the practice of true love.

Obviously, the ideal is not to have begun this practice of true love
by chance in one's last hours. It would be better to reach it without uselessly prolonging the delays. In fact there are countless people
who very early in life, love with God's love. We meet these people in
all kinds of situations.

The total acquiescence of their being to the impulses of divine
life aroused in them by the grace of their baptism is expressed by
their simple acceptance of the natural interplay of existence and
the difficulties with which it is inevitably accompanied. They love
without phrases, demonstrations, psychological analyses, or explanations. Thus, they give without even thinking a total direction of their
whole being to the Holy Spirit who lives in them. God assumes every-

thing in the lives of these simple people—the accomplishment of humdrum tasks as well as the highest responsibilities.

The purity of the testimony given thus by those who belong to all walks of life lets us understand that the success of a human existence is not bound up with the accomplishment of the dream that each one may have had about his own times, other people, or himself. Success depends wholly on the availability that the Holy Spirit will have found in him to the gift of loving. In this is the true success of an existence.

Far from having wasted himself on short-lived satisfactions, man, through his availability to the Holy Spirit, is destined to a going beyond that he was called to accomplish with his fellowmen.

By placing himself thus under the guidance of the Holy Spirit, man comes to love with the love of God. When one loves in this way, he does not seek to impose himself on another. He does not seek to give them any illusions about himself. He is incapable of deceiving the confidence they have placed in him. Knowing and accepting one's own limitations, one gives them as a guarantee of security only what one is really able to give them in fact.

When we love with the love with which God loves we give to the other real possibilities for self-expression. We do not interrupt them at the first stammer or at the first contradiction they utter. Whether it be on the level of individual exchanges or on the level of relations between one collectivity and another, love consonant with God's love creates for the benefit of all a total possibility for self-expression.

When we love with the love with which God loves, we are faithful to the other. To the end, we will believe in the other and have confidence in his possibilities. In difficult hours we never use pressure tactics by saying we are disappointed. This would be to testify against oneself by admitting that, in fact, one did not love the other but only the dream *in* him about self with which one had become infatuated.

When we love with the love of God, we have respect for the freedom of the other that is one with our own availability to the Holy Spirit, for it is to the same Spirit that we are subject whether in another or in ourselves. We know that to diminish or to meddle with the freedom of another, even to confirm him in that which we think to be his own good, would be to make more difficult his own self-transcendence.

The only freedom that we will consider limiting or reducing is that which we would have the right to claim for ourselves (cf. 1 Cor. 9, 1-24; Rom. 14, 1-15).

Conclusions: True success for everyone is to know how to love.
"Love others as they are without desiring for thy sole advantage that they be better Christians," wrote Francis of Assisi in a letter to one of his brothers.

This is to love with a love like the love of God. It is with this love that the Holy Spirit wishes to love within each baptized human heart, within the heart of all humanity, that heart which is the Church.

Perhaps to understand this well it was necessary for the Church, as for each Christian to have been a father or mother. One is a father or a mother when one has known what it is for another to choose his own destiny. This is necessarily a painful experience.

Even the Virgin, who had given birth without suffering to the Son of God made flesh, was not able to become without suffering the mother of men who are subject to the determinisms of the flesh.

But this painful experience teaches man the only science that is indispensable to be fully a man; that is, to be disposed to enter into COMMUNION with God, to know how to love.

All the solicitude of God for us is exercised in this direction; it is for us to cooperate with the Holy Spirit who dwells in us (cf. Rom. 8, 2), to render possible this achievement of our being. Individually, as for all humanity, it is the true achievement, the one in view of which all else must be ordered.

FIRST REFLECTION ON THE THEME
Submitting Ourselves to the Spirit

A. POINTS FOR MEDITATION

1. To learn to love is the essential apprenticeship of existence.

2. To love truly is impossible for him who has not discovered others as persons, whether through friendship, or married life or through the human relationships of education or the service of others.

3. The success of a family or community is determined, above all, by the quality of the love that is lived therein. To this quality a thousand imponderables contribute, but these are all ordered to the mutual knowledge of persons.

4. The first effect of a true love is to free us in regard to ourselves, but it can occur that a love, true in its beginnings evolves toward withdrawal into self. By refusing to be purified through the expansion of its relationships, that which began as liberation becomes degraded into enslavement through selfishness.

5. To love God with a pure love cannot be an end that is sought by a sinner.

6. Sexual realities approached sanely and in their human totality are the normal road to a real understanding of intimacy with God. In particular, man receives from the behavior of woman in regard to love a capital lesson. There can be real intimacy with God only at the price of a self-giving to God without self-seeking. The joy of being loved by God is experienced only after having made in FAITH the abandonment of one's being to God's will.

7. True religious and priestly chastity is not contempt for love. It is, on the contrary, a greater esteem for it. It is, above all, an intuition through grace of the possibility of having a more complete access to true love through a more perfect availability to persons in whom the will of the Lord is manifested.

8. The feminine world is dangerous for the priest and the religious only if they forget that their mission is to encounter in it only persons. One no longer seeks to encounter only persons when one is led by the need to be admired, understood, pampered, etc.

9. Many sexual problems are, in fact, signs of far deeper prob-

lems one has refused to confront. It might be a lack of maturity that one will not admit to oneself, a realization of disappointing limits, the consciousness of failures that are not understood, the refusal to integrate into one's life such and such a person or element that is of necessity a part of it, or the nonacceptance of self. These are all, as a matter of fact, refusals to love. These refusals have their repercussion in all of man's being and upset the balance even of his biological structure.

10. There are collective refusals of love. Many problems that form themselves on the level of human groups or of the human group in its totality are in fact signs of these refusals to love. Divisions, oppositions, wars outside and revolutions inside of countries, the shock of warring ideologies and subversions are facts to be taken into consideration not for themselves but to discern a deeper evil of which these facts are the consequence. They are refusals to love to the degree that they are collective refusals to organize human life on the basis of love. These refusals express themselves habitually in instinctive reactions of collective individualism of class, nation, race or continent. These reactions have their repercussions in the life of the human group and upset its balance even in its economic bases. There is no need to have recourse to the devil in order to explain these convulsions of humanity. The refusals to love (both conscious and unconscious) are a sufficient explanation.

11. The consciousness that the refusal to love is at the beginning of all the disorders of existence can make the Christian understand how the grace of his baptism makes him a leaven of liberation and human progress in his environment and through this environment in all of human society. This consciousness must cause the Christian to desire as a supreme ideal the freedom that is submission of all his being to the Holy Spirit.

12. Modern life is characterized, among other things, by a paroxysm of the sexual; one has been able to speak of pansexualism. The specialists of the different sciences of man examine this phenomenon to discover its meaning. They all recognize the part sexuality plays in the formation of the person. At the same time, however, they denounce man's total absorption with sex as the consequence of an insufficient orientation of the human dynamism. The great task of those who must enlighten men seems to be to throw light on this orientation because without it, man would destroy himself. His

dynamism would be deprived of its true object. It is for scientists to promote the discovery of this orientation from their research into the reality of man.

The Christian knows what this orientation is from revelation. He has been told that he is made for LIFE. The only end in which his dynamism can find its fulfillment is in loving and being loved with a perfect love, the love with which God loves. To refuse systematically to recognize this destiny of man because it is supernatural can only be prejudicial to him. One cannot distort human reality without dire consequences, in view of the end for which he was made. Blocked on the road by which he was to reach his full expansion, man is condemned to all the maladies through which the disarray of a vital dynamism deprived of its real pole of attraction expresses itself. Cancer of our innermost being is expressed in the display of eroticism as well as in the secret perversions revealed by psychoanalytic investigation.

The best thing that society could attempt would be to seek to see the connection between the refusal to recognize the supernatural and this unhealthy situation. The best thing that the Church could do would be to show men through acts what it is to love.

"HE WHO HAS SHOWN IN OUR HEARTS"
(2 Cor. 4, 6).

A. From the awakening of religious feeling to the taking charge of our being by the Holy Spirit.

Speaking of Israel through the mouth of the prophet, Hosea, God says:

"I led them with cords of compassion, with the bands of love . . . and I became to them as one who eases the yoke on their jaws . . . and I bent down to them and fed them" (Hos. 11, 4). There is in this text a description of the tactful steps by which God makes himself known to man ". . . it was I who taught Ephraim to walk, I took them up in my arms" (Hos. 11, 3).

It is in everyday life on the occasion of the most humble and even humdrum situations that is set in motion in man, even if he ignores it, the process that is to lead him toward the entry into communion with God.

In all the situations man lives, God is instructing him, and every step man takes that lifts him above material determinisms (devotion to duty, the fight for justice, the search for beauty, the cult of truth) is, in fact, a step taken by God to draw man to himself by making man desire him (cf. 1 Cor. 2, 9).

Of all these approaches of God working in man the most common as well as the most elevated in the natural order is that which the human being experiences when he awakes to love. This happens, first of all, when he experiences the love with which his parents surround him and then by his experience of the love that is represented by the founding of a home and the bringing of new beings into the world.

This last experience is certainly the one through which the human being is the most deeply and totally approached by God; both his flesh and his spirit are engaged in it. From this approach all humans will normally benefit through the simple unfolding of the laws of nature. But above these laws there is an approach of a more

185

elevated, more total and wholly gratuitous order of which the human being is the object when God through some motion of an irresistible character draws this being by a personal and wholly interior attraction (cf. Mt. 19, 11; Jn. 6, 44).

Thus, we have the concert of attractions with which God works to make man emerge from the womb of the created. Wonders of beauty in flowers or wonders of cohesion in the constitution of matter, wonders of tenderness encountered in others, or wonders of the inward attraction that inclines a being to desire nothing outside of the Most High—these are instances of the divine attraction exercising its power on man through the varied interplay of the satisfactions of nature and the attentions of grace.

But man, when he enjoys this, is exposed to the danger of resting in the satisfactions that he experiences. He can imagine that these satisfactions crown his worth, lend authenticity to his own value, and sanction the part he plays or the position he fills in life. "But they did not know that I healed them" (Hos. 11, 3). When man turns the solicitude of God into satisfaction with self, the result is detrimental to him. What man must do in the course of his existence is to grow, to increase in stature, to go beyond himself, to enter finally into the full flowering of his being in a completely new life.

Nothing is more fatal to the growth in us of this new being than to imprison and immobilize ourselves in satisfaction with some aspect taken on by our being in the unfolding of its becoming.

There are complacencies in this reality of self that are the gifts received from God through nature, youth, strength, intelligence, beauty, position, and social status. There are also complacencies in the reality of self that are the gifts received from God through grace, knowledge of and intimacy with him, and aspirations toward and service of him.

From the first type of complacency God delivers us through the action of existence. All through our lives there are given to us the necessary purifications—advance in age, the trials of ill health, reversals of fortune, and bereavements and separations. The second type of complacency is far more difficult to detect and to avoid, for it is founded on spiritual motives. God intervenes personally in our existence to make possible through his own authority these liberating purifications. They are the work in us of the Holy Spirit.

B. Purification of our being through silence and by listening to the word of the Holy Spirit.

Through the grace of baptism the Holy Spirit comes to "dwell" in us.

He becomes thus inside of us a power of animation for the renewal of our being. In other words his life, animating our conduct, substitutes itself in us the life that comes to us only from the "flesh" and that, originating in matter, confines and limits our life and our aspirations to horizons limited by matter (cf. 1 Cor. 11, 10ff.; Rom. 8, 5-14).

This action of the Holy Spirit in our being does not depersonalize us, for it works wholly in the direction of the full realization of our being. It is the force of attraction coming to join the self-propelled energy of the rocket so as to launch the satellite into orbit.

This taking charge of our being by the Spirit gives us access to the life of the Spirit, SPIRITUAL LIFE. "It is to your advantage that I go away, for if I do not go away the Counselor (Holy Spirit) will not come to you" said Jesus to his disciples (Jn. 16, 7).

It is good for every man that the experienced and enjoyed presence and solicitude of God came to an end. Then there came to humanity the presence of the Holy Spirit mysteriously constructing the Church. When God becomes absent there begins for the individual the mysterious direction by which the Holy Spirit will make of him a new being, a son of God.

To make our direction effective the Holy Spirit will remove every good in which we have the weakness to be complacent and he begins this work in our senses, our imagination and our intelligence.

Who has not known the classical condition in which, while we may feel in the best of form for any kind of work with our mind full of ideas for discussion and writing, yet as soon as we try to put together several thoughts or feelings in mental prayer we find ourselves regularly with an empty head and a dry heart?

Let us understand properly the meaning of this inner condition. It is a reappearance in us and for us of the history of the people of Israel. Let us remember God calling his people to a purified cult, refusing the holocausts and all the sacred "butchery" in which Israel so manifestly found satisfaction (cf. Ps. 50, 7f.; Ps. 51, 18ff.). As the true Israel, we are invited to detach ourselves from the satisfactions that we find in our successes in prayer.

But this renunciation is neither spontaneous nor easy for us. We are so attached to the idea, as Israel was, that we are giving something to God, so God ceases to lend his cooperation to an activity in which we offer him a cult that he no longer wants from us, and our faculties so alert for every other occupation find themselves paralyzed when it comes to prayer. Just as a mother obliges her child to be silent when it has grown too old for her to be content with its repetition of mere words, so the Spirit of God imposes itself on our spirit and reduces it to silence.

In this, above all at the beginning, we experience a painful impoverishment. We want so much to continue to feel something or to be able to say something! Now this experience of impoverishment is essential to the accomplishment of the going beyond that is our destiny as children of God.

In regard to the created, man knows no practical limits to his power; he can dominate the cosmos from one end to another, from the secrets of the atom to the depth of the galaxies, from politics to depth psychology. All this is in the created order, man is its fruit and also its living conscience taking charge of his own foundations.

On the contrary in his going beyond that he must accomplish to come to the uncreated, man is totally incapable of self-sufficiency. He cooperates on this journey only as a conscious and voluntary material that lends itself freely to the power of the Spirit who alone can make a new being (1 Pet. 2, 5). Without the Holy Spirit, man can elaborate all sorts of technologies, philosophies, and even all imaginable theologies. He cannot without the Holy Spirit elaborate one good thought. Only the Holy Spirit can draw from the depths of his being a cry of true FAITH, a movement of authentic hope, an impulse of real charity (cf. 1 Cor. 12, 3; 2 Cor. 3, 5; Jn. 15, 5).

It is thus that the same man (cleric or layman) can animate the reflections of a group of Catholic Action Volunteers, direct souls, and assure their spiritual instruction all the while that he finds himself empty, dry, and brought to nothing whenever the hour comes for him to assume his own period of prayer and meditation.

C. By reducing us to silence in prayer the Holy Spirit leads us to the reality of existence. We must understand properly the significance of this reduction to silence in the life of prayer.

The Holy Spirit pursues and completes therein the experience that man gains from his advance into existence.

Difficulties of life, obstacles and failures, aging and loss of health are silencings on whose occasion our being learns to detect its limits in action. Beyond these silencings in action the Holy Spirit makes possible for us a silencing in repose. This experience is essential to our entry into the truth of our relations with God. Effectively, man experiences his incapacity to accomplish that which in appearance requires the least personal effort—to converse with God.

It is hard to admit this incapacity because here there is no possible alibi. One can, through agitation, give oneself the impression of doing something. One cannot even by tormenting one's mind or one's sensibility produce from them the thoughts or impulsions of the heart that the Holy Spirit will not give us to elaborate in them.

It is normal then that we are tempted to avoid the trial by ceasing to pray. There are so many good reasons not to waste one's time doing nothing!

Now to persevere in prayer despite the abject state to which this silencing has reduced us is an indispensable condition of our progress in the spiritual life. Through this state the Holy Spirit delivers us from an illusion that is more fallacious than the illusion of action, for here there is brought to nothing all pretensions to give to ourselves communion with God through some refinement of our minds (imagination, sensibility, or intelligence).

The religious man is naturally inclined to mistake his fervor (impulses of the heart, fine ideas, etc.) for "signs" that God is with him and favors him. Israel also took as signs of the favor and approbation of God the enrichments of the periods of Joshua and Judges. In fact, these enrichments were only the fruit of rapine and theft. Rapine and theft are like every prayer in which man is complacent and every union with God is weighed according to satisfactions of the sensibility, the imagination, and perhaps according to the successes of an intelligence full of theological thought. The silencing of these faculties is an occasion for us to detect the ambiguous character of our fervors. At the same time, the silencing is the means used by the Holy Spirit to bring us back to the realities of existence, for it is in the realities of existence that we must accomplish the self-transcendence to which it tends, the entry into communion with God.

When in prayer, the source of images, movements of the heart, and thoughts are manifestly exhausted, it is important to discern the call that the Holy Spirit is addressing to us through this inner condition.

To persist in trying to extract from one's brain or sensibility some word or impulse soon becomes exhausting. Worse still, these impulses and words will be so empty of meaning that we will have the impression that we are lying. Distractions and temptations will descend on us in the course of our prayer like wasps on a pot of jam. At any rate, this is above all, not the time to forsake prayer.

But we must lend ourselves to the action of the Holy Spirit who knows how to remake in us this life of prayer from the realities of our daily lives. "Sow for yourselves righteousness . . . Reap the fruit of steadfast love . . . break up your fallow ground . . . for it is time to seek the Lord" (Hos. 10, 12).

Sowing, harvesting, clearing new ground—these are the actions to which we are called by the Holy Spirit. They will preserve the life of prayer from being depraved into the search for a "god" who would only be an inner "idol" tranquilizing us in the satisfaction experienced by an exclusive possession of it: "God and myself"!

The solicitude of the Holy Spirit who dwells in us is therefore exercised on our being in the way most appropriate to our real needs. Reducing us to silence in prayer, he brings us back to action and from active situations, he causes new demands for prayer to spring up in us. This is to say clearly that the taking charge of our life by the Holy Spirit does not demand structures of life that are any different from those normal in every human life. In particular the dialectic of repose-activity that characterizes human existence is to be found on the level of spiritual life in the dialectic of prayer-action. There is no truly human life without a display of activity. If nothing is done, there is only delay and even regression. There is no truly human life either when there is no relaxation in repose. The inextinguishable need for holidays felt by modern man is the irrefutable proof

of this. Authentic life according to the Spirit, except for those un-
usual situations for which the Spirit is free to provide in his own way,
will develop itself in an authentic human way where serious activity
and true repose alternate harmoniously according to the aptitudes,
temperaments, situations proper to each individual.

Then, there is no longer opposition between prayer and action,
between mental prayer (presence of God) and involvement in activity (presence to the world). Life according to the Spirit is lived just
as well in activity as in the repose of prayer; the Spirit alone is the
master of those who have surrendered themselves to him.

Conclusions: Communion with the Father through the restoration of true freedom to our being.

The surrender of our being to
the Holy Spirit puts us therefore
in the position to assume all the
realities of our existence as divinizing realities.

Action as well as prayer, everything of which our life is composed
is matter for the elaboration in us of the new being promised to glory.
In this dialectic of prayer and action the Holy Spirit makes it possible for us to be aware of his divinizing action. This awareness flowers
into a state of habitual union with God, *the life of prayer.*

The expression, "life of prayer," wonderfully expresses the reality established in us by the Spirit. In the life of prayer we come face
to face with God. (The Latin word, "orare," means to express oneself through one's face: that is, through one's entire attitude.) In this
encounter, our inner countenance is illuminated by the face of God
(cf. 2 Cor. 4, 6). The face of God is easily identified and lovingly
adored in the innermost depth of each situation that is lived and in
the depths of one's own personal being.

To attain this end, all have here on earth an equal chance. The
philosopher and the theologian are in no better position for this than
the last of the humble. For that which comes to the wise at the end
of a long detour marked out with analysis, the simple and humble
can attain directly by accepting in their totality the conditions of life
that existence has given to them. Although their ways are different,
they achieve in the end to the same result. In the one as in the other,
man is no longer fearful. The face to face encounter with God has
ceased to be formidable for him. What should he fear from God?
Not only does he, in taking charge, leave him his complete freedom,

but he sees from day to day that this taking charge of him makes him more and more effectively free. After such an experience one knows vitally that to become fully oneself is to abandon oneself.

Life's realities can then be welcomed with the fullness of consent that is given to a human being by the consciousness he has of his own freedom. Our times, others, ourselves—everything becomes an occasion to enter into COMMUNION with divine ACTION. In all these realities, our being led by the Spirit discerns and adores the will of a God who is a Father. Everything becomes an occasion to love with the love with which God loves.

In a letter addressed to his brothers, Francis of Assisi prayed the following to his Father in heaven: ". . . that inwardly purified, inwardly illuminated and kindled by the flame of the Holy Ghost we may be able to follow in the footsteps of this Son our Lord, Jesus Christ." (Letter to all the Friars)

Francis of Assisi gives us here a summary of the work of the Holy Spirit in us. This work results in making us free beings who are capable of following Jesus Christ. Beyond all the stages we have passed since the initial energy that has taken created life from inferior to superior states, this is the ultimate passage, the entry into the life of the Father. "It is the Spirit that gives life, the flesh is of no avail" (Jn. 6, 63). From the corruptible, the Spirit elaborates the risen Jesus Christ in us; we make the passage to the incorruptible (cf. 1 Cor. 15, 45-46. 53-54). With Christ, even here on earth, we can say with the Spirit, "I thank thee, Father!" (Lk. 10, 21.)

SECOND REFLECTION ON THE THEME
Submitting Ourselves to the Spirit

A. Points for Meditation

1. The desire to know God is innate in man, but the search for this knowledge is fatal to man if it degenerates into a will to know or a will to perform. Lack of moderation always destroys in man the germ of the true entry into the knowledge of God. God can be known only through the way of communion to his LIFE, that is, through loving.

2. To love is neither to possess another, nor to reduce another to an object. Nor is it to be possessed and reduced to an object oneself. It is to enter, one and the other, into a current that is neither

from self nor from the other and that carries both toward an end that is transcendent.

3. The current that carries us along is that of divine life communicated to men by Jesus and the Father, sending their Spirit into the world. Present in the world (in the heart of man and at the heart of the life of men), the Spirit who is love channels the entire human world toward the realization of the mystical body, the ultimate end of the created universe.

4. To love with the love of God can be given to a man only at the end of a long, rough, and often painful search for the truth about himself. An entire human life is sometimes spent before one knows the exact dimensions, often very selfish ones, of what he had thought was true love.

5. An important guarantee of purity in our relations with others is to love with the intention of giving consideration to others (those who are the most different from ourselves) as an indispensable act toward our own completion in Christ (cf. 1 Jn. 3, 18.21).

6. The following are discreet manifestations of a true love. Experience as much joy in hearing said by others that which one knows, as if one had been the first to reveal this news oneself. Feel as much satisfaction in learning from others as in teaching them. Marvel as much before the riches and qualities discovered in another as when these are discovered in oneself.

7. The respect for another's freedom is not only a contribution to the personal entry of the other into communion with the Father. It is the entire universe that is called to love and to live the Father's life. It is therefore for the entire universe that the Christian must desire and obtain freedom.

8. Marxism has made evident the alienations that prevent man from being himself. The Christian must not be slower than the materialist to denounce and combat these alienations. But he knows that in this combat, he must work according to the Spirit, for only the Spirit of God can free man entirely from the alienations that are the direct consequences of sin.

9. The consciousness of this task of liberation to be accomplished and of its true requirements cannot be possible without silent reflection thoroughly penetrated by adoration. We are dealing here with the mystery of the life itself of God that is to be established in man.

10. This silent reflection steeped in adoration does not neces-

sarily require a retreat from all activity among men. There are no outward structures indispensable to the action of the Spirit in us. The one indispensable condition is fidelity to the reality of human life in prayer and action.

11. The heritage of Jansenism lies not only in the rigorism of moral life; it is also in every attitude that refuses to recognize the place of salvation in the manifestations of human life.

12. Bodily health, calm of the senses, moral and mental health, inner silence. The more one lives and loves with perfection, the less one wastes oneself by saying that one is living and loving.

B. Texts for Reading and Prayer

a. Biblical Texts

Ezek. 11, 14-22; 37, 1-15: Promises of the Spirit.
Joel 3. Prediction of the wonders operated by the Spirit of God and poured forth on all men.
Job 4, 12-21. Experience of a face to face confrontation with God.
Jn. 7, 37-40; 16, 5-15. Jesus announces the coming of the Spirit.
Acts 2; 11, 15-18. Effusion of the Spirit.
Rom. 5, 5; 2 Cor. 1, 21-22; 5, 5. The gift of life in the Holy Spirit.
Rom. 8; 12, 1-15; 14; Gal. 5, 13-25. Life according to the Spirit.
1 Cor. 12, 1-14.39. The gifts of the Spirit.
Rom. 13, 8-15. Primacy of Charity. Compare also Cor. 13.
Eph. 1, 3-14. The revelation of the plan pursued by God explains all things.
1 Jn. 3, 4. Testament of the disciple Jesus loved.

b. Books

St. Francis, *Rule,* 1, chap. 22; *Admonitions.*

c. Prayers

Slowly meditate, in short stages, the lines of Psalm 119. This text of meditative prayer is characterized by a contained joy. There is identification between living and being faithful to the Lord. One can return with profit at this point to the three stages of the Second Step.

Final Theme

1 Jn. 5, 21.

III

Transformed into the Image of
Jesus Christ

> "Lord . . . may I feel in my heart as much as
> possible that love without measure with which you
> were inflamed, you, the Son of God, and which
> led you to suffer so much pain for us sinners."
> St. Francis

["HE] HAS SHOWN IN OUR HEARTS
TO GIVE THE LIGHT OF THE KNOWLEDGE
OF THE GLORY OF GOD . . ." (2 Cor. 4, 6).

A. To become conscious of the fatherhood of God in mystical experience. The adhesion, without any reservations, that our being gives to the entire will of God proceeds from a consciousness: in the "face to face" encounter with God, our being, inhabited by the Spirit, recognizes itself as living the life of God.

We must underline the supernatural character of this discovery made in the innermost recesses of our being. This discovery is a free gift; we do not make it of ourselves.

Even without the determinisms of sin, our being would have been incapable of conceiving the true dimensions (supernatural) of the passage to which God was calling it (cf. Eph. 1, 17-20).

Man has always dreamed of going beyond this universe his destiny. But he has never imagined this going beyond as anything but an improvement, a sort of "new edition" of life here below, or as a return to a great impersonal "ALL" or again as a simple taking possession of the cosmos by a superhumanity that is to come.

Now while it is brought back to the realization of its own incapacity through the silence imposed upon it by the Holy Spirit our

195

own spirit, that is, the innermost depths of our being, discovers in the face to face encounter with God the true going beyond to which it is called by God. It cries out, "Abba . . . Father" (cf. Rom. 8, 15; Gal. 4, 6). In this simple phrase is expressed the consciousness of the true self-transcendence we are called to accomplish.

We are able to become aware of this because of a reality that it already acquires—our own divinization. For our parts, there is a consciousness supported by the Holy Spirit of the paternity of God.

Let us insist at once that the paternity of God is not the distant and general sort of paternity which the best pagans had foreseen and which philosophers define beginning with the act of creation. This is a personal paternity; the Person of the Father is recognized personally as father by the human persons we are.

If my spirit in calling to God employs the term, "abba," it is not at the price of extending the meaning of this term; it is because in the depths of itself my divinized being lives and experiences the reality of the personal relationship of filiation to God. Thus, the small child experiences and lives the reality of his condition as a son when he cries, "Father," to him from whom he expects everything.

To express ourselves thus in our relations with God might seem to be unbelievably audacious (cf. Eph. 3, 2-22; 2 Cor. 3, 4).

The contemporaries of Jesus understood very well the absolutely unprecedented, new and unique character of the relationship with the Father that Jesus claimed for himself. To address his Father, Jesus did not employ the usual term—the very exact equivalent of our own expression "our Father." Jesus used the word, "abba," a term that had for his listeners the same tone and the same childish boldness that for us is contained in the word, "daddy." Now it is this same term, "abba," that the Holy Spirit, joining himself to our own spirit causes to rise from the depths of our own being. The experience of our own divinization is expressed in this cry.

Such an experience can be understood only by those who have undergone it. Already, on the level of the created, all that is life is at the same time mystery. One does not understand life because one has analyzed it, but because one has tasted it.

This is all the more true on the level of the uncreated. The realities lived therein are impenetrable to anyone who has not personally experienced them. It is in this sense that they are called mystical realities.

For many Christians, mystical life evokes a collection of wonderful happenings of the order of the miraculous. In fact, mystical life can exist outside of any wonders at all. It is even the most frequent case. Many people lead true mystical lives without knowing it. Their lives differ in nothing from the lives of those who live around them. But in the innermost depths of their being they bear the living experience of that transcendence to which God calls them.

B. Mystical experience leads our being to desire total adhesion to the will of God.

Mystical experience is the practical awareness (and therefore not necessarily analytical) of the transformation of our being in its depths, at that central point where our intuition of reality and our personal will are expressed.

One day, a young girl becomes conscious of the fact that she is loved by the tall young man with whom, since her childhood perhaps, she has always been friendly. The love that was at work for many years in the depths of her being suddenly erupts into consciousness on that particular day. Outwardly nothing is changed, but from now on, all is transfigured and happiness is to abandon oneself to this love. This experience can be that of the great majority of human beings. It should at least be that of all those who are married. In this experience, one finds the image that comes closest to allowing us to understand the mystical experience.

In the mystical experience, a person, through some event lived on the level of consciousness, experiences that he is loved and desired by God. Outwardly, everyday life may remain rigorously the same as it was, but all realities are henceforth transfigured. Happiness is to abandon oneself to God who loves.

Mystical experience is personal. It is therefore always lived in an individual manner. But all mystical experience is a participation in the mystical experience lived collectively by all humanity, in fact, in the historic event that was the coming of Christ into the world.

After hundreds and thousands of years of simple neighborly relations between humanity and God, humanity has had the experiential consciousness of knowing itself to be loved by this God that it had feared. Christ is at one and the same time the place, the instrument, and the expression of this consciousness, and since Christ, this consciousness is prolonged and developed in the Church that is the mystical consciousness of humanity.

In Christ and in the Church, the world experiences that God is personally engaged in all that makes up the reality of its history. The world discovers that its own total achievement is inseparable from a total adhesion to the will of God. All the natural dynamism of the world can come to will itself in the direction of God's own will.

This mystical experience, at once unique and total, that is, Christ and his Church, constitutes the decisive event in the history of humanity. Nothing is changed in the exterior conditions of human life; man is born and grows, he struggles and suffers, works and dies. But in its depths humanity is transformed. In the measure of its own collective adhesion to the will of God the mystical body of Jesus Christ is elaborated in it. This is its own perfect fulfillment.

Each individual mystical experience is a participation in the unique and total mystical experience that Christ and the Church are for all humanity. In individual mystical experience, a man becomes conscious that God is personally engaged in his life as a Father. In individual existence as in the history of humanity, mystical experience is the decisive element. Having become aware of his own divinization, the human individual sees his own personal achievement as inseparable from a total adhesion to the will of God. All the natural dynamism of this man will be willing itself henceforth in the direction of the will of God.

Mystical experience is indispensable to the entry of man into the perfect accomplishment of himself just as the mystical experience of the incarnation in Christ and the prolongation of the incarnation by the Church was indispensable to humanity. As long as man fears that God will alter or diminish his being, he lends himself only with reservations to the attraction exercised by God on his being. But when man has experienced that the attraction exercised by God on his being is for his fulfillment, this satisfaction, once experienced, makes him will himself to be in a total adhesion to the will of God who fulfills all his desires.

It is the Holy Spirit who makes possible in our being this liberating conversion and he testifies in us that this conversion has been effected when from the innermost depth of our being; causes us cry out, "Abba, Father" (Rom. 8, 16).

In making us call God with the name of Father, in the very sense given to this name by Jesus Christ, the Holy Spirit testifies that we are really sons. In the Spirit we are truly born to the life of the Father (cf. 1 Jn. 3, 1).

C. Adhesion to the will of the Father subjects us with Christ to the total reality of existence.

To be born to the life of the Father is to be born to life with Jesus.

Only the Son knows the Father because only the Son is born of the Father. He who is born with the Son to the life of the Father becomes also with the only Son a son of the Father. And in the Son he also knows the Father. The realization of the transcendence to which we are called is summed up in this, that we must be born with the Son. It is evident that to be born with the Son cannot come from ourselves. No one can give himself another's life. How much more is the life of the Father a gift! We can be born with the Son only through the free action of the Spirit.

But at the same time that it is a totally free gift escaping our wills, this life of the Father cannot be established in us without our willing it. We are born with the Son to the life of the Father by communing with all of our being to the conditions in which the Son of God came into being as son of man.

Jesus Christ lived his human life as a man. He was taken for a man by those who saw him live. This is to say that in everything that makes a being a man Christ behaved as a man (cf. Ph. 3, 7). He did not pretend to be a man. He accepted in its totality the reality of human existence.

In this reality, there is the law of matter. The technician knows that he can dominate matter only by submitting himself to it in accepting just as they are the laws of its internal constitution and the qualities that derive from them, such as weight, resistance, solidity, and elasticity.

There is also the law of life. The peasant learned long ago to respect the different stages of growth and the rhythm of the seasons.

There is finally the law of man. Man learns every day that he cannot take his destiny into his hands without submitting himself to the truth about himself—the total truth including his fallen state because of sin. To accept this reality is the only way not to be bewildered and disappointed.

The Son of God made man accepted this triple law of matter, life, man. He bent himself to the reality of matter; at his work bench he applied the rules of his profession. In his development, he was acquainted with growth and with waiting. Above all, he applied himself to the reality of man; he accepted without refusal all the elements of human life.

To be born with Christ to the life of the Father requires of men that they live the totality of human reality as did Jesus Christ who is Son of the Father and the perfect realization of man.

Mystical experience lived in a unique way in the Person of Christ is continued collectively in the mystery of the Church and is repeated personally in the life of each Christian who aspires to the perfect accomplishment of his destiny as a child of God. But the authenticity of the individual mystical experience is, first of all, evaluated by the normal insertion of the Christian into the entire human context. This authenticity is subject to caution the moment there occurs need for exceptions or freedoms in relation to the normal demands of reality.

The mystical experience does not set an individual apart. It makes him free in conditions common to all. It makes man capable of ENDURING enough to be able to accomplish freely what he would have a right personally to refuse to himself. Suffering and death, humiliation and solitude cease to be for him a fearful fatality. He knows that he is not subject to these things because of a punishment whose law would have been directed against him. He knows and wants himself to be subject to them as a contribution that is required of him in order that there be reestablished the equilibrium of the living environment in which the human being, individually and collectively, can then have access to the ultimate and superior form of being that is life in communion with the Father.

Conclusions: Mystical life consists essentially in the total adhesion of our will to the will of God.

It would be regrettable for Christians to relegate mystical experience to the domain of the exceptional, if not the unbelievable. Mystical experience awaits every Christian. It gives access to true inner peace whatever one's situation in life.

Starting from this experience, life, in its activities as in its periods of repose, becomes a filial presence before God, who is recognized as living and acting everywhere. It is an habitual and peaceful state of loving attention to all the manifestations of the Kingdom of God in the world around us as well as in ourselves. The possibilities of ACTION, purified of that which altered their value, pass more and more completely under the influence of the Spirit who dwells in us. Docile to his motions, able to respond effortlessly to the expectations revealed to us through our relations with others, we are, in a certain manner, given back to ourselves in the gift that is made to us of being able to love perfectly (cf. Eph. 3, 17; 4, 30).

In the man who is thus reconciled with God (cf. 2 Cor. 5, 20) and with the universe (cf. Wis. 5, 21), there is established even here below the true peace promised by the Lord (cf. Jn. 14, 27).

Spiritual writers of the Eastern Church have given to this modality of being the name, *apatheia,* and they have seen above all in this state a serene repose that becomes possible for man when his surpassing of interior troubles is the fruit of his ENDURANCE.

St. Bonaventure, as a good Western spiritual writer, has given to this modality of being the name, *sursumactio,* and he underlines by this word the activity expressed in this condition that has finally been delivered from the confusion with which sin had marred it.

The diversity of expressions corresponds well to the diversity of the modes of life in the Greek East and the Latin West. But it is the same experience that these two apparently opposite terms designate.

The most frequently used term in the West to designate this modality of being is the word, "contemplation." It is important not to give a restrictive sense to the word "contemplation." This is done all too often when contemplation is identified with a particular attitude closely related to retreat from, or even refusal of, action.

Christian contemplation is not a type of life. It is a modality of being, a new manner of perceiving, of feeling, of thinking, and acting where action as well as thought and the perception of the world are transposed to an entirely different level. ACTION and ENDURING are informed by a total grasp of things, the grasp that is given to man by true knowledge of God. It is experimental knowledge, the gift of the Spirit who dwells in us and makes us sons of God (cf. Gal. 5, 22).

Contemplation is lived in action as well as in repose. It translates itself with predominances that are proper to the diversity of temperaments and cultures into action as much as into prayer. Above all, it is not linked to any particular condition of life, for this would end in making it the lot of a few privileged souls when it is in fact received in germ by all in the grace of baptism.

Action and prayer join each other in contemplation to deepen in us the consciousness that God alone is all in all and that all exists only in accordance with the thought and loving will of a God who is known as a father.

St. Francis, broken by illness, was asked by one of his brothers if he would not have preferred to die a martyr by the hand of some executioner. Francis replied "Whatever it may please my Lord God to have happen in me and with me has always been and still is most dear, most delightful and most acceptable to me. For all I desire is to be found always in agreement with his holy will and obedient to it in all things."

Such a state of being is the fruit of the action of the Spirit in the heart of man (cf. 1 Cor. 2, 12). To lend himself to this action is the real victory man must win. In it, man triumphs in Jesus Christ over the most dangerous of human pretensions—the pretension to accomplish the transcendence to which his being tends by a way other than living according to the reality of human existence and in loving. Thanks to the mystical experience, man strives with men. A new Jacob overcome by God, he too can say: "I have seen God face to face and I am not dead" (Gen. 32, 31).

FIRST REFLECTION ON THE THEME
Transformed into the Image of Jesus Christ

A. POINTS FOR MEDITATION

1. We know God in loving with the love with which he loves. To love with the love with which he loves is given to us by the Spirit who has come to dwell in us, and make of us sons of God. The

awareness of this gift is the decisive event of both collective and individual human life.

2. The mystical experience does not make a man disdainful of human values. It is, on the contrary, the salvation of these values. It situates them in their rightful place, neither an end nor a center but a stage of development to be lived for a going beyond that is to be accomplished. It lets everything be ordered to this going beyond because it denounces the false glamors in which sin is continually imprisoning us.

3. An evangelization that would limit itself to finding and hailing human values without bringing these values to submit themselves to the image of Christ would not reach the transcendence that must be accomplished. These values must recognize in Christ their example and their origin, the indispensable instrument of their achievement and the final term of their own flowering.

4. It is not for us to fix a price on human values that are recognized by the world as a sort of payment for salvation. To do this would be to persevere in the error of a dialogue with God in terms of a balance sheet. A new moralism is established (to the benefit of non-practicing Christians). But salvation is not a favorable balance at the end of a column of figures; it is entry into LIFE. This entry presupposes on our part a conscious and personal adherence to the plan of God who in Jesus Christ has wished to introduce us into it. "He who believes shall be saved."

5. The Church is not a world apart. It is neither a refuge for him who wishes to flee the world nor a moral élite claiming to guide the world. The Church is the mystical experience of the world, the consciousness by men of the action of the Spirit guiding the universe to its completion, the response of men to this action of the Spirit especially in the recourse to the sacraments.

6. The Latin Church so rich in individual mystics has not sufficiently recognized the importance of the mystical experience in its collective life. The realities of ecclesial life are formulated in it in terms of law and administration much more than in reference to the action of the Holy Spirit in the consciences of men. To relegate the mystical experience to the domain of the exceptional can only be prejudicial to the authenticity of Christian life and of missionary expansion. "That which we have seen, heard, touched with our hands" (1 Jn. 1, 1).

7. The Latin spirit in the Church is not only expressed in terms of law; it is also expressed in the heritage of Roman roads, and in oratory. Such solidity can only escape disease by the proliferation of the mystical life.

8. When mystical life is depreciated, the preponderance of institutions is not only translated into an administrative and juridicial view, it is also expressed in the priority given to techniques. Many who promote liberation from institutional rights can become the artisans of a new enslavement in regard to the structures of evangelization.

9. Religious life is, above all, walking in the footsteps of Christ. The true prosperity of religious life is therefore linked to the authenticity of the conditions of the human life in which it is expressed. Mystical life perishes, and religious life weakens when for the conditions of normal life are substituted conditions of life made easy through the elimination of the problems of human existence.

10. To soundproof a cell or even an entire convent will always be a technique. To achieve silence in the depths of one's being and as a consequence, in a given place, will always belong to the domain of mysticism. Silence is only worth that with which it is filled.

11. A thousand voices arise in man, capable of stifling in him the sighs of the Spirit (cf. Rom. 8, 26). Not to reduce these voices to silence is as fatal to the love with which God loves that is come to dwell in our hearts as was fatal to Christ when he came to live on earth the cowardice of Pilate in front of the crowd. One does not establish an exterior Christ before one is not yet in an attitude of adoration interiorly.

"IN THE FACE OF CHRIST" (2 Cor. 4, 6).

A. To live human existence in reference to Christ introduces man into participation in the Passion. To be born with Christ to the life of the Father demands therefore that we live the reality of our human lives as Jesus Christ, perfect image of man, lived this reality. This is why the adhesion we give to the will of the Father is ultimately an adhesion to the image of Jesus Christ.

Seen by the Apostles (cf. 1 Jn. 1, 1-3), engraved in their memory (cf. 2 Pet. 1, 15-18), transmitted by word, gesture, and attitude, the image of Jesus Christ has introduced into the darkness of the visible the splendor of the invisible (2 Cor. 4, 6). In the face of Christ humanity has seen the shining glory of the beyond to which it tends (cf. 1 Pet. 8; 2 Pet. 1, 16-19). This image is henceforth at the point of convergence of all the human impetus.

In his sacred humanity, the Lord Jesus Christ is at once the obligatory model (evangelization) the indispensable instrument (sacraments) and the unique finality (mystical body) of all perfect human accomplishment, as much on the individual as on the collective level of all humanity. Between the world of humans (the result of the entire labor of the universe) and the communion in the life of the Father, the sacred humanity of Christ is the only way. We must live all the situations of our own life in reference to it.

Our present times have deepened in humanity the awareness of a human condition situated in space and in time. In space we know the place that is held by our terrestrial globe; it is one of the tiniest grains in the cloud of dust that is the cosmos. In time, man, thanks to history, manages to identify himself in the course of an evolution of which he is conscious of being, in a way, the final product at the end of millions of years. This awareness would lead man to anguish and insanity if he did not dominate it by the certitude that he has of being on a road that leads to a transcendence. Now this certitude so necessary to man is more and more cruelly lacking to him. Former certitudes seem to grow ever smaller in the measure that man, through his investigation of the universe, pushes back their limits.

Lost in an immensity without shores of infinite space and in his own inner questionings, man longs for unity within himself and for unity with all of reality. He needs a total vision gathering together everything in a unique light.

This total vision is a unique light given by the Word of God made flesh when this Word made flesh, Christ, enters into the silence of a passion and death that are finally resolved in the transcendence of the resurrection (cf. 1 Cor. 15, 20-28).

In the prologue to his *Journey of the Mind to God,* St. Bonaventure spells out the requirements: "There is no path but through that most burning love for the Crucified . . ." This master of the spiritual life, the inheritor of Francis of Assisi, does not intend to leave the Christian confined to the meditation of the passion as an event of the past. On the contrary, he wants to invite him to take for himself with an ardent love the condition lived by Christ on the cross as a normal condition of life for the Christian. How, in fact, can one pretend to be born oneself in the Word to the life of the Father otherwise than according to the conditions that this Word assumed here below, and continues to assume in the mystery of his Church? He lived the "days of his flesh" under the burden of sin. He can live in us the days of our flesh only under this same condition beneath the burden of the sins of others, of course, and also the burden of the sins of our times and of the times that preceded us. But above all, he lives in us beneath the burden of our own sins, no matter who we are or may be. It is this that we are unwilling to admit because we are humiliated by it. To love the crucified ardently engages man in the silence that is a participation in the passion.

B. Participation in the Passion reveals to man the "silence" in which is expressed the acquiescence of his being to the will of God.

Every man, to the degree that he has to live the life of a man, finds himself one day or another to be concerned with the passion. It is the day when tormented by the most fundamental questions man can no longer give to himself any other reply but that which is the face with the closed lips of Christ.

As a child the human being asks his interminable "whys" and he accepts without sifting through them the replies of his parents. In his youthful days the human being questions others and questions himself. Henceforth he rebels against any answer that does not satisfy in depth his need to know. As an adult, the human being sees questions rising from every side. He notes that there are questions to which nothing or no one gives even the beginnings of an answer.

Man begins, then, a dialogue that is an entry into contestation with God. It is frequent for discussions to become conversations between the deaf; only words are exchanged in them. But an attitude, a simple gesture can then express our true depths better than any formula.

In reply to the questions of man, God has made himself gesture and attitude, the face with the closed lips, of the passion and death of Jesus. In this passion and death, the innermost being of the Lord is expressed just as it is informed by the love with which the Father loves; the depths of divine life are revealed. It is there when he is silent that Christ becomes for us most truly the living Word of the Father. In the silence of his passion and death, no human words, or formulas that can lend themselves to interpretations are present to form a screen or a veil between him and us. He speaks to us face to face, from the depths of his being to the depths of our being. His silence is the last step in which, Word of God made flesh, he communes with the reality, heavy with sin, of our human condition. And the state of prostration to which he has allowed himself to be reduced is the reply of his heart to all the questions which existence causes to be born in our hearts (cf. Mt. 26, 63).

Now this silence of Christ on the cross takes up again the first question made by God to man: "Where are you?" This silence of Christ on the cross is a true question addressed to every man. Through this silence man, the questioner, brought back to total reality is reduced to entering into a similar silence.

This "similar silence" to which we are reduced by the Word of God living out his own death is situated far beyond the silences that the Holy Spirit had already imposed upon us in action as well as in prayer. These silences were only an apprenticeship, a progression. The passion introduces us into the most total and purifying of all silences—the silence of being.

Beyond the purification of our different faculties that the Holy Spirit provides for us in action as well as in prayer, there remains to be lived the purification of this innermost being in us that finds its expression in the act of loving. This purification is made possible for man when the conditions of life that are his lot condemn him in a way to express through refusal, revolt, and even hatred the very depths of his being that only wanted to express itself in love.

This was the situation lived by Christ in his agony. He whose whole being only tended toward love had to fight within himself to be able to accept being rejected by his own people without ceasing to love them.

We who are called to love must live this situation. It is all the more necessary because sin is in us and weakens us. It is all the more terrible because our condition through the sin of others is weighted down with a burden of more inhuman ENDURING. Does it not often happen that this endurance is caused for us by those from whom we had the most right to expect that they help to lighten our burden for us—churchmen, for instance?

When it comes to assuming such a reality there can no longer be question of words because there are no longer any words that ring true. The Word of God reducing itself to a loving silence teaches us that we can be true ourselves only by living this reality in a loving silence. But for our being that is divided and weakened by sin, this attitude can be reached only at the end of a long and difficult road. More often than not, it is only possible to arrive at it after one has struggled painfully to come to grips with oneself in the midst of swirling eddies that are made up of refusal, revolt, and even hate.

Many men ignore the real meaning of these eddies when they endure them; they see in them a sort of condemnation of themselves, above all of their pride, when there is lived in their being through these struggles a real participation in the agony of Jesus. This participation is far more authentic here than in the often purely verbal and superficial adherences that we give to situations that present us with no difficulties.

It is thus, for example, that unbelief on the part of certain individuals or social groups can sometimes be the expression of a participation in the agony of Jesus that belongs to mystical experience. On the other hand, such and such a form of belief may express only a fruitless religious life. There must be years of struggle for the individual (and many generations on the collective level) before the innermost part of a being who wishes to love finally reaches the expression of a *fiat* that is worthy to be associated with the one pronounced by the Lord. The authenticity of such a *fiat* will be recognized in that its natural expression will be silence, when from the depths of our being there will cease to rise both protestations of pain and superficial proclamations. We will then have entered the silence of being, a loving silence.

It is through participation in the passion of Christ that man learns this silence. It becomes evident here that to participate in the passion is, above all else, a state of conscience. Participation in the passion is not a simple softening of the heart. Neither is it a devotion (in the modern sense of this word). Nor is it a function which one will have chosen among many others that were offered in the life of the Church. Above all, it is not the attribution to oneself of a certain quota of discomfort or suffering to be endured. To participate in the passion is to live with the will to assume one's human condition in all its truth, that is, one's own self, others, the times in which he lives without avoiding or eluding any of the abasements to which his existence makes it a duty for him to subject himself. There is no question of creating sources of suffering for ourselves. It is enough to welcome in silence and to bear lovingly all the unpleasant things that result from the original disorder of sin, each time that it would be possible for us to avoid them only by letting them weigh or fall upon others.

This is what St. Bonaventure calls "that most burning love for the Crucified" (*Journey*, Prologue).

C. To enter into loving silence restores the unity of our being and we become open to the action of the Holy Spirit. It is not easy, nor does it come spontaneously to man (even to a religious) to place thus above all reasoning and practical proofs the Word of God as it is formulated in the silence of the passion and death of the Lord, the CRUCIFIED WORD (cf. 1 Cor. 1, 18; 2, 16).

Preparation is indispensable so that a reflex that is so far from natural to us can be educated. This preparation is made slowly. At its beginning, it demands the humble step that consists in meditating on the passion of the Lord during a time long enough to end in an habitual remembrance (cf. Gal. 3, 1-2).

It is always prejudicial to skip this step. Whoever will not consent to oblige himself to it will have difficulty in arriving at communion in the sufferings of the Lord (cf. 1 Pet. 4, 13). He who does oblige himself to it will, on the contrary, find his reward on the day when the images from his own life fuse with those of the passion. Everything that is hardest to live is seized and lived in the heart of Christ (cf. Phil. 1, 8). Far from crushing or destroying us, suffering then introduces us into the loving silence that places all of our being under the guidance of the Spirit. Active and fruitful as it is, this silence of being allows us to live the present to the full without wasting it in any way through words or spasmodic reactions of defense however painful may be the trial to be endured.

Such a silence is not the privilege of money or of culture; it is not determined by implantation or by the materials out of which our house is built; it is compatible with modern activity, with the most deafening of noises at the factory and with the animation of a fair or exposition. It is a permanent communion with the passion and death of the Lord accompanied by the certitude of his resurrection (cf. Phil. 3, 10-11). This silence, accessible to all, is the only silence that is indispensable to the perfect achievement of man for his entry into communion with the Father.

The living Word of God made flesh, Jesus has fully told man all that he came to tell him only by accepting to make himself silent through death on the tree of the cross. The passion is the condition of life through which the "Word-of-God-made-flesh" attains in relation to the sinners that we are the most perfect expression of himself. Nowhere else does God ask man as clearly the essential question, "Where are you?" (Gen. 3).

To this living Word of God, man is himself an answer. In man, it is the whole universe brought out of nothingness by the creative Word which attains in a certain way its ultimate self-expression. But this reply of the created universe that is man cannot attain in relation to God its ultimate and perfect expression individually as well as collectively unless it also accepts to formulate itself through silence—the silence of a life lived as a participation in the passion of the Lord.

"It is I who will reestablish my Alliance with you . . . that you may be reduced to silence when I will have pardoned you all that you have done," says the Lord. Jesus, hanging from the cross in "participation to the human condition," is the Word of God to man (Rom. 5, 8). Man, entering into silence in participation to the passion of Jesus is the reply of the universe to God. The RETURN of creation to God is no longer impossible. Man can tear himself away from the determinisms in which sin had imprisoned him. For this to happen it is sufficient for him to be in communion with the opprobrium of the cross (cf. Heb. 13, 12-15).

It is through this state of communion in the death of the Lord that so many poor people without culture have had access to contemplation without even knowing it. They knew Jesus poor and crucified. One does not enter into this superior mode of thinking and acting because one has disciplined one's physical and mental faculties, nor because one has sharpened one's speculative intelligence. One enters it because one has embraced Christ on the cross as the only complete answer to all of the questions that can be born out of life.

The man who "carries thus the death of Christ" (2 Cor. 1, 5; 4, 10) sees established within himself the true inner unity that is PEACE and definite CERTITUDE. Unity in man is artificial as long as it does not stem from the concentration of all the dynamism of our being by a unique image capable of surviving every accident and every disillusion.

In the state of contemplation that is established in us by participation in the passion, all the dynamism of our being is focused on the image of Jesus poor and crucified. There is no question here, except at the beginning, of a material image evoking such and such a scene of the passion but of a spiritual image gathering together the inner states of Jesus in his silence. In the light of this image, our being is able to discern in every situation that it must live a preparation or rather an element of its own Easter and the universal Easter. Beyond its own interior convulsions, our being, in the unity of the sacred humanity of the already glorified Lord, lends itself to the Holy Spirit for the consecration that the Holy Spirit pursues in it throughout all things. This consecration encounters no more resistance in us than it does in the bread and wine that on the altar become the body and blood of the Lord. Through the action of the Spirit our being is made eucharistic in its everyday life just as all humanity is made eucharistic by becoming the Church.

Conclusions: The restoration of the unity of our being gives us access to the fullness of joy and peace. "Our Father most holy," cried Francis of Assisi, "that we may love thee with the whole heart by always thinking of thee; with the whole soul by always desiring thee; with the whole mind by directing all our intentions to thee and seeking thy honor in all things; and with all our strength by spending all the powers and senses of body and soul in the service of thy love!"

In this paraphrase of the *Our Father* Francis reveals his own interior state of unity of being to us.

By communion with the "interior states" that are expressed by the silence of the Lord, this interior unity that was broken by sin is completely restored. Nothing is desirable to us anymore but that which our very holy Father wants from us.

One can then arrive at finding as much joy through the accomplishment in ACTION of the great desires that torment us as one does by ENDURING the burden of situations that make their accomplishment impossible. Often it is in the second of these states that the knowledge of God grows the most deeply. ACTION itself is, as it were, absorbed in a naked enduring. Man finally arrives at loving himself for what he really is—a pure relation to a God who is a Father and who through his WORD engenders him continually in the interior of his created work and his own uncreated life.

Through this awareness, man identifies in God in some way the real source of all his being. He can henceforth only adhere with all of his vital forces to the thought and will of God on him. All the freedoms of which he could avail himself will be used to espouse the will of God. It is in this sense that man becomes, so to speak, incapable of sinning. The very idea of sin makes him shudder. The image of sin is as intolerable as would be that of self-destruction. Sin is no longer fled from as from the alteration of an image of self that one loves; it is fled from as an attack against the plan that God is pursuing in ourself and in others. One abhors and hates it like a true death; it is a refusal to the Father who creates us, to the Spirit who enlivens us, and to Jesus Christ who is formed and grows in us (2 Mac. 15, 18).

Thus are there reopened for man, even here on earth, the true sources of joy. These sources of joy, symbolized in Scripture by the four rivers that irrigated the earthly paradise (cf. Gen. 2, 10), had been closed by sin. They have been reopened by the passion of Christ whose wounds pour forth their lifegiving flood of waters on the desert that is sinful man (cf. Jn. 7, 37). For the man who enters into participation in this passion, Eden is restored. This man discovers again the transparence of all things (cf. 1 Jn. 1, 7). Once more a child (cf. Mt. 18, 1-5), he no longer feels the need to hide (cf. Gen. 3, 10). He is no longer afraid because in him, love has become perfect (1 Jn. 3, 19-20; 4, 17-18).

Thus is the term to which leads a life lived in participation to the passion of the Lord. It is already the paradise on earth, the perfect joy announced by Francis of Assisi to his brother Leo.

In this light, the word of God that is for man this world and his existence in it (himself, others, his times) is no more in any way a word of discord, for nothing any longer is said to man to which he cannot lend himself with love. Everything reveals a God who is a Father. Death itself becomes a sister because it appears as the breaking of the last link that prevents our entry into the fullness of freedom, that is, the fullness of life and love.

To obtain even here below as much as is possible this entry into plenitude, it is worth the trouble to seek the "face of God," which is "the face of Christ," with our whole being (cf. Ps. 27, 8). But to do this we must know how to be silent long enough to allow Christ, the living Word of God, to express himself silently in our existence.

Reduced to silence in action, reduced to silence in prayer, man will see the face with the closed lips portrayed in the depths of his own being as in the depths of the being of his brothers. He will know how to expect from Christ the accomplishment of his own perfection in the accomplishment of the perfection of all humanity in the Church.

SECOND REFLECTION ON THE THEME
Transformed into the Image of Jesus Christ

A. POINTS FOR MEDITATION

1. The transcendence to which God calls man is the birth of a new world in which man is a new being. This is necessarily painful, for it is like that which was endured by Christ, the living Word of the Father.

2. This way to the knowledge of God is summed up on the face of Christ Jesus as man's condition here below allows him to be seen, that is, attached to the cross.

3. The participation in the passion is first of all a communion to the inner states lived by the Lord. It is presumptuous for us to assume that by allotting to ourselves a certain quantity of sufferings and mortifications, we can become worthy of this participation. But it is just as presumptuous to count on this participation without welcoming and even, if need be, imposing suffering upon ourselves. Suffering that is welcomed causes us to enter into deeper communion; deeper communion makes us more inclined to welcome suffering. Communion feeds on suffering that is endured, and suffering becomes sweet and even desirable through communion.

4. "Always suffer, never die . . ." was the cry of St. Teresa of Avila. In her this is neither morbid masochism nor ascetic falsity. It is the deep awareness that her life of trial was a participation in the passion of Jesus. She knew the joy of knowing oneself to be engaged in one's personal achievement through generous contribution to the accomplishment of collective destiny.

5. Through participation in the passion, the Christian dies with joy to every self-made image of himself. His being is totally directed towards the one image of Jesus Christ (cf. Col. 3, 1-4; 10-11. Rom. 8, 29).

6. Through participation in the passion, Christians are collectively delivered from the temptation of trying to obtain the triumph of such and such an image of the Church that is dear to them. Only this participation in the passion makes the Christian capable of avoiding different forms of triumphalism—the triumphalism of temporal glory, of liturgical splendor, but also of service and that of

destitution. The participation in the passion frees us from enslavement to our own interior constructions and places us at the service
of the possibilities with which the human reality of the moment is
pregnant. Far from thwarting or hindering the action of the Spirit,
we are ready to let the Body of Christ take on the traits that the Spirit
wishes to give it.

7. The participation in the passion frees the Christian from the
triumphalism of service by making him prefer the slow pace and
the stresses of true obedience to the glamor of services rendered with
a view to bearing witness.

8. The world of today and of tomorrow as did that of yesterday
expects Christians to contribute to its scientific and technical endeavors. But the more the becoming of the universe goes toward
its final end, the more must this contribution of Christians take on the
form of a participation in the passion of the Lord. In other words,
the more the development of this becoming allows one to have a
presentiment of its term, the more will Christians consider it their
duty to bring their contribution without banners or trumpets.

9. The worst obstacle to the entry of unbelievers into FAITH
is the triumph that would be celebrated over this entry by those
who imagine themselves to have FAITH.

10. The Church has always known, but churchmen always need
to learn again, the economy of salvation. The Chinese priests who
are reviled and reduced to lap their food from a bowl with the slug-
gards, the Christian activists who were sent to the gas chambers with
the Jews, the nuns raped and flogged to death in the Congo in vengeance for abuses committed by others—these are of greater value
for the salvation of the world than the mightiest technical or cultural achievements of which Christian organizations may have been
able to boast. Christ saved the human world by burying himself in
it at the lowest level of the human condition, the level of the common criminal condemned to death.

11. The most subtle triumphalism is the triumphalism of destitution. The Christian will guard himself against this triumphalism by
remembering frequently that the death of Christ on the cross is an
event on the order of a "news item." The importance of this
event for the salvation of the world comes from the inner dispositions
that were those of our Lord.

12. When it is the fruit of a true participation in the passion, the

inward attitude of adoration can become so connatural to man that it invades the totality of his being. Without any prejudice to the unfurling of his own dynamism in various activities, this man sees established in himself the state of loving lucidity that is contemplation.

B. TEXTS FOR READING AND PRAYER

a. Biblical Texts

Is. 62, 1-9; 69, 1-7; 50, 4-9; 52, 13-53; 12. These texts, in describing the Servant suggest the way for every man to follow if as a true Israel, he wishes to allow himself to be led by God into LIFE.

2 Cor. 3, 18—5, 8. Paul describes how he lives this experience of the action of God inside himself.

Phil. 3. The only thing that Paul wants is to know Christ by conforming himself to his sufferings, to be part of Christ in his glory (cf. Phil. 1, 21).

Is. 60; 62. Proclamation to our human being (represented by Zion) of the wonderful restoration reserved for it by God.

b. Books

Thomas of Celano, *Vita Prima* Part I, chaps. 28-29.
St. Francis. *Rule,* 1, chap. 23; *Admonitions.*

c. Prayers

Is. 42, 10-17. Song of victory addressed to God the Master of events.
Pss. 22; 31; 35. Try to pray these psalms by situating yourself in the drama lived by Jesus attached to the cross.
Pss. 93; 96; 97; 98; 100. Homage to the all-powerful God who saves.
Is. 61, 10. The song that will be on our lips at the time of the "revelation" of the sons of God.
St. Francis' Office of the passion. In the text of this prayer, composed by St. Francis from fragments of scriptural texts, one notes his inspiration. He does not attach himself to scenes belonging properly to the passion, but lives in depth the inner conditions of the humiliated Christ and responds to them with his entire soul. Compare the Canticle of the Sun. Here we can return with profit to the three stages of the third step.

Final Theme

Rom. 15, 7

Conclusion

Since the days of Adam, God has called to man, "Where are you?" It is always the same question that falls on man's ears. To understand this question that comes to him through his own personal nature, other men, and his own times, he must be silent and attentive.

Individually or collectively, man will be wholly attentive only when "he looks upon the propitiatory and turns his face fully towards the Crucified" (St. Bonaventure. *Journey* 7, 2). "I am," Christ has said, "the way, the truth and the life" (Jn. 14, 6).

He is the way: a way that must be taken even if the end to which it leads is not distinctly seen. We must follow Christ by participating in his passion just as he has participated in our human condition. For the world of men to end in glory, it is demanded of us that we consent with Christ to endure the sufferings which accompany our belonging to a moment of the march of this world. It would be useless for the men that we are to desire to hold the key to our destiny as a condition for its acceptance. On the other hand, man does hold this key as soon as his participation in Christ's passion makes him enter into the reality of life as into a preparation for glory.

He is the truth. By his words and even more by the silences of his passion, Christ uncovers the lie at the bottom of every will to success that fails to recognize the essential rule of human existence: Thou shalt love. This will to succeed while despising love is denounced as the prolongation of the refusal to endure that has upset the balance of the human condition. Action becomes exclusive of all else while it pursues those false victories in which man dehumanizes himself into a superman and dehumanizes the human group that he has the time to form according to his idea. On the other hand, whoever is possessed by love with Christ crucified attains his own personal unity and makes the collective unity of people advance according to the truth.

He is the life. In him and by him man has access to the life that con-

217

sists in knowing the Father. He who knows Christ, that is, he who accepts to be born with Christ to existence by espousing the inner states of mind that were his is born to the life of the Father. Through a necessary participation in the passion of the Lord, he sees accomplished in himself and allows to be accomplished in others the PASSAGE from this transitory world to the new world where, in Christ, the Father will be all in all because all those who live the life of the Spirit will henceforth be in perfect COMMUNION with the Father (cf. 1 Cor. 15, 28).

You wish to LIVE. Be attentive to the Word and you will understand. The Word is not far away; it is in your heart; it is on your lips without your paying any attention to it (cf. Deut. 30, 14).

The Word tells you that there is no other life but his, who alone is LIFE. All life is only a preparation for death if it does not go beyond itself so as to enter into true LIFE, in view of which it is made.

Learn therefore to recognize the invisible, to recognize in your own life as in the existence of your fellowmen the inner dynamism that tells you where everything is directed. The SPIRIT of God is there; he is working in you and in the universe. Lend yourself to his action (cf. Jn. 1, 18).

Do not remain outside of this enterprise to which all that is in you that is authentic wishes to take part, for it is Christ.

And to do this, consider all your own enterprises and discern in them that which is preparation and perhaps realization of God's eternal enterprise (cf. 1 Pet. 1, 2).

The Lord Jesus comes. And in you as in the world, the same cry is launched toward him by everything that truly exists and lives: "Come, Lord Jesus, come" (Rev. 22, 17.20).

Friend, reader, my brother, baptized son of God, I permit myself to beg you: "Formulate this cry, lend your voice to it, and above all, your life!"

In this way you will have taken part in the "mystery of history" and will have entered into the "mystery of God," in the TOTAL CHRIST, a mystery of LIFE and LOVE.

Text: 1 Pet. 1, 3—2, 12.